Travels with Mensans

ISBN: 978-1-84753-340-1
First published 2007. Published by Lulu.com

About the Editors

Neil Matthews was born in London and lives in Buckinghamshire. He is a Chartered Marketer by profession. Neil joined Mensa in 1992 and has edited VISA, the newsletter of British Mensa's Travel Special Interest Group, since 1995. This is his first book.

Barry Needoff was born in Manchester and lives in London. With a Master's degree in Tourism from the University of Surrey, he has worked in travel industry information technology since the late 1980s. After joining Mensa in 1990, Barry became one of the first members of British Mensa's Travel Special Interest Group, and has been its Secretary since 1995. This is his first book.

**MEDECINS
SANS FRONTIERES**

Net proceeds from the sale of this book have been donated to Médecins Sans Frontières (MSF). MSF was founded in 1971 by a small group of doctors and journalists who believed that all people should have access to emergency relief. MSF was one of the first nongovernmental organizations to provide urgently needed medical assistance and to publicly bear witness to the plight of the people it helps. Today, MSF provides assistance to populations in distress, to victims of natural or man-made disasters and to victims of armed conflict. MSF relies on donations from the public for two key reasons: to ensure the freedom to provide humanitarian assistance whenever and wherever it is needed, and to remain independent from political, religious and economic interests. Your help is as valuable to MSF as that given by our field volunteers - without it our work would be impossible. Your support demonstrates solidarity with the people MSF helps: "When someone points a gun at you and asks 'who sent you?' I can answer that it was people who care. This can mean the difference between life and death." (MSF logistics specialist Steve Hide)

Thank you for your kind support of our work in buying this book. For more information, visit www.msf.org.

Introduction

Travels with Mensans owes its existence to Mensa, the High IQ society, and specifically British Mensa's Travel Special Interest Group (SIG). The Group, and its newsletter *VISA*, brings together Mensans with an interest in travel to share their impressions, experiences, opinions and, above all, their enthusiasm. Some of the best writing published in *VISA* has been included in this book.

The articles you are about to read were not specially commissioned, nor were they written for tourist authorities or travel service suppliers with interests in any of the destinations we have included. The writers contributed to *VISA* because they wanted to share their thoughts, their experiences and their reactions to the places they visited. *Travels with Mensans* gives you the chance to read those thoughts, written in evocative and sometimes provocative style. It has been a great pleasure to re-read them all in the preparation of this book.

We are extremely grateful to all the contributors for agreeing to the re-publication of their words and pictures; to Derek Trillo for supplying a superb collection of additional photos; and to Richard Kingston for founding Travel SIG. We would like to thank Sara Zaffino of British Mensa for her hard work over many years in collating and distributing *VISA* to members of Travel SIG; John Stevenage and Bobby Raikhy, also of British Mensa, for the Society's agreement as publisher of *VISA* to the re-publication of these articles, and for their ideas and encouragement; and Brian Page, editor of *Mensa Magazine*, for running his experienced editorial eye over our collection. Thanks also to Pat Bensky, Andrew Dunham, Sylvia Herbert, Rowena Love, Jane Mason, Susan Reid, Susan Watkin and Michael Watson for additional advice; to Stewart Kennedy for his help; to Janice Booth for proofreading; and to Helen Matthews and Jenny Stuart for their ideas, support and understanding during the preparation of the book.

There is a popular, much touted view that the world is a smaller place than ever before. We hope that this collection helps to put the opposite view. The unprecedented growth of travel and tourism has brought home just how large our world is: and so much larger, and so much stranger, and yet so much more fragile, than ever.

Neil Matthews & Barry Needoff
Editors, *Travels with Mensans*

Contents

Asia & Pacific

Children's Palace, North Korea (photo: Neil Harris)

The Laos Incident
John Keeble (1999)

For a few seconds, everyone froze into a strange tableau; the old Hmong woman, wrinkled and bent, perhaps her grandson with his son, a few passers-by and lingerers, the internal immigration officer who had just told us that the rules had changed and that she didn't need to clear us to leave the town, the *jumbo* driver with his confident air and smart reflective shades, and us.

It was one of those moments when the modern world collided with the traditional world: perhaps a moment when, at the grassroots, something shifted for ever for those dozen or more people in the old royal city of Luang Prabang in central Laos.

The incident began with me photographing the woman as she squatted by the pavement selling small bags of firewood, some embroidered squares and a crude metal bracelet. In return, she wanted a sale. She held up two fingers for 2,000 *kips* for the bracelet, no doubt expecting to sell for 1,000. The driver of our *jumbo* - like a *tuk-tuk* but larger - said something that astounded her and then turned to my wife June and me, and said the price was 10,000 *kips*.

Every head turned. Everyone froze. Would we pay ten times the going rate? Oh, sure, why not? She needed it. We didn't. I handed over the money and took the bracelet. She was stunned. Everyone gawped. All over £1.50. And it was suddenly clear what an amazing ride many Lao and hilltribe people were going to have as Western commerce, tourism and media took off in the emerging Divine Kingdom.

You do not get that kind of experience in Vientiane, the capital, where 10,000 *kips* would be enough for a *jumbo* driver to grab your arm off. But we were travelling through Laos from the west, an unusual way into the country at the moment, and people there have not had time to catch up with the ways and opportunities of the *falangs* (*farangs* for "foreigners" in Thailand, *falangs* in Laos where our 'r' is not part of the language).

We flew up to Chiang Rai in northern Thailand from Bangkok and took a bus to the frontier town of Chiang Khong, where we bought our visas through an intermediary for $60 each. The next morning, a light mist over the Mekong, our ferry edged across to Huey Xai with us and half a dozen backpackers. We went through the formalities, exchanged £100 for a huge wad of 660,000 *kips*, and got a *jumbo* to where the fast boats were moored.

They were not exaggerating, I thought, as the fast boat rocketed off along the Mekong in the direction of Luang Prabang. The stylish, brightly painted rowing boat with a car engine bolted on the back was fast - from 0 to 50 in seconds. But, what the hell, if you don't like living on the edge, don't travel to strange places with nothing but your bag of essentials and some cash. Our essentials, as it turned out, included a copy of the *Triple Gem*, a very readable introduction to Buddhism that we bought in the hill tribe museum over the Cabbages & Condoms restaurant in Chiang Rai: it helped us decode the imagery of people and architecture alike.

We could have gone down the Mekong in a slow boat. It takes two leisurely days to cover the 300 miles to the World Heritage town. But women are not allowed on the cool roof lest they confuse the senses of Buddhist men and that takes the edge off the experience. So we joined a Dutch couple and hired a fast boat. Six hours, plus one for a pitstop with noodles. Within minutes, the thrill of speed gave way to the interest of river life and the unfolding scenery, jagged hills fading blue to grey, until, thanks to the vagarious nature of the Mekong's course, we arrived at Luang Prabang as the sun set in front of us - as near as a fast boat gets, anyway. From there, it was another 20 miles of dusty roads before we arrived, battered and dishevelled, at the best hotel in town, the Villa Santi, which was once owned by a princess and which usually takes well-groomed guests who arrive in a limousine from the airport.

We emerged from the Villa Santi in the mild air of the February morning to explore its historic area between the confluence of the Mekong and Khan rivers. The temples date back to the 16th century but almost every one has been destroyed and rebuilt at some time as Laos' violent neighbours - especially the Siamese, Chinese, and Burmese - have invaded and withdrawn. Xieng Thong is the classic Luang Prabang *wat*, with its distinctive deeply-sloping roofs, its royal funeral chapel (housing an enormous funeral carriage holding royal ashes guarded by a dramatic *naga*, Buddha's seven-headed serpent so loved by Lao temple designers) and a unique reclining Buddha. We sat in the shade, looking at the chapels and *chedis*, the ripple of the blossom, and the slow and dignified passage of the monks.

It was there, in Xieng Thong's tranquillity, that we met Sing Thong, a 16-year-old novice. He was waiting for someone who would help him with his English grammar and, lesson over, he showed us around the *wat* and told us about his life. Later, we went to his 6ft x 8ft room, which he shared with another novice, and drank tea while we talked. He wanted to be abbot of Xieng Thong, one day, after he had travelled and maybe studied in Thailand.

On the other side of town was Wat That Makmo, better known as the Water Melon Stupa. The temple houses a breathtaking collection of valuable and historical Buddha images. The shutters of our cameras clicked: were we paying our modern respects or collecting a little of the eternal peace of That Makmo? Maybe both.

Most people who visit Luang Prabang make the journey to the Pak Ou caves, with their 4,000 Buddha images. They travel the 25 miles by boat but we hired a *jumbo*. It was a hilariously bad ride that we wouldn't have missed and the trip included June earning her rice by taking up the good-natured challenge of women road workers to help dig foundations. UNESCO, in its citation for Luang Prabang's elevation to World Heritage site (with the consequent inflow of much needed restoration money), said the town uniquely blended Lao and French colonial influences. Its laid-back atmosphere, open-air eating places that lure you into gluttony and the warm people make it easy to simply enjoy the legacy of the past without reflecting on the horrors that the people have seen: from the US bombing campaign to civil war and the imprisonment and deaths of the king, queen and the last prince less than two decades ago.

We left Luang Prabang in a clapped-out coach on the notorious Route 13. The coach was better than the people-carrying truck that was the alternative and it carried a mechanic because everyone, including us, expected it to break down. It did. Twice. The second time, the transmission fell out and the crew worked heroically as nightfall approached. They say Highway 13 is safe now that the army has moved in but until four years ago, Hmong guerrillas were carrying out raids with automatic weapons. We saw no soldiers and heard, while waiting for the bus to be fixed, only the hauntingly beautiful sound of a woman singing as she worked in the wilderness of the high hills.

Vangviang, two-thirds of the way to Vientiane, must be among the world's most beautiful places. But not when we arrived at midnight with everywhere closed and the streets black. We managed to find a family with rooms to let and we slept: room, bed, shower, kindly concern - £1.80.

The town, which feels more like a village, is built in the sweep of the Nam Song river, with endlessly enticing views towards the horizon of limestone crags and hills. Those hills offer a dozen interesting caves and caverns - we opted for a distant cave and hired a motorised ox-cart. A point at my flip-flops and a universal "OK?" brought a warm affirmative from the driver. It wasn't that he didn't understand me: it was just that he thought it was quite OK to climb 650ft up boulders, some sections almost vertical, in flip-flops. But the effort was well rewarded: the great cavern and, in a pale light from a higher opening, a 20ft reclining Buddha.

The bus down to Vientiane was crowded. But it did not prepare us for the maelstrom of the city. The bus station was a seething mass of people and vehicles. And the city roads, in the rush-hour, were just the same. Eventually, in yet another *jumbo*, we arrived in the green haven of Villa Manopy guesthouse, with its antiques, quiet service and UN residents. The city centre was dusty enough to make breathing difficult and it had none of the easy-going friendliness of Luang Prabang. But, beyond the centre's scrum, there was the charm of gentle places and gentle people.

Pha That Luang - the Great Stupa - is where Buddhism and the state fuse, the former legitimising the latter and the whole becoming the symbol of nationhood. Its golden form encodes Buddhist doctrine from statues at ground level to the central spire, a stylised lotus bud symbolising the growth of the person from the mud of ignorance to the sunshine of enlightenment. We climbed the steps into the monument and later sat in the serene, walled grounds for several hours. A monk walked by and smiled; a family were harassed round by a tour guide; a young couple idled away half an hour. But we saw no one else at this, the country's premier monument.

It was like that wherever we went: a scant few people walked round Xieng Khuana - better known as Buddha park - with its dozens of concrete sculptures of Buddhist and Hindu gods and other figures, one more than 50ft tall. And at Sok Pa Luang, the forest *wat* famous for herbal saunas, we were the only *falangs*. The people at Wat Si Muang, the busiest temple in the city, welcomed us during their day of making merit by taking gifts of flowers, incense, candles and fruit. June made merit by releasing two tiny birds from a cage and a young novice, Boun Thone Siamphone, gave us bananas and cut coconuts so we could drink the milk.

Si Muang is the temple where people go to make wishes. If their wishes are granted, they must return with gifts of fruit. When we return, we shall take bananas and coconuts to Wat Si Muang. The wish fulfilled and the gift delivered at the same time.

4

Trans-Siberian Express
Helen Krasner (1999)

There are some fascinating overland trips in the world. I know; I've done a number of them. The train from Lima to Huancayo in Peru climbs to over 10,000 feet in a few miles, with scenery to match; trips in the African bush are a photographer's delight; the route to India via Afghanistan and the Khyber Pass I remember from nearly thirty years ago.

The Trans-Siberian Express from Moscow to Irkutsk in Eastern Siberia is not one of these trips. It is a journey that is far, far better to have done, than to actually do. Anyone who tells you otherwise is lying, spent the whole three days drunk on Russian vodka, met some fascinating people, or is completely turned on by trees. And trees, and more trees, and still more trees. They were planted by the railway to stop the snow, but the result is you can't see beyond them, for the best part of three days and nights.

Of course, there are compensations. You stop at stations, strange towns apparently in the middle of nowhere, where exhausted travellers wander up and down, buying hard-boiled eggs and *piroshki* (pies) from old ladies in headscarves. There's the obelisk marking the border between Asia and Europe, where everyone gets out their cameras. And one day there was a rainbow, and the whole train went completely berserk, a little like an Andy Warhol movie when a fly crosses the screen after eight hours of nothingness.

Moscow, to which we flew from Heathrow, had been wonderful. We were met at the airport and whisked off to our host family's flat in Moscow's centre. Their 15-year-old son spoke excellent English and we were provided with a guide who was quite happy that we preferred to sit in the park and quiz her about life since the break-up of the USSR, rather than visit the Kremlin. Then the epic train journey began.

In Irkutsk, after this memorably monotonous journey, we were met at 4.30am, and driven straight off to a village on Lake Baikal. Again staying with a family, we sunbathed by the lake (I recommend Siberian summers, and have the suntan to prove it), took boat-trips, tried out our hostess's Siberian sauna. Then came a couple of days in Irkutsk, a lovely town full of old wooden buildings, with a definite Mediterranean feel. I had to keep reminding myself that this area has nine months of snow, and buying a holiday cottage there really wasn't practical.

On the last day we had an amazing thunderstorm - pink forked lightning and rain that topped the wheels of cars and almost completely stopped the traffic. Our driver, determined to get us to the station, had to be forcibly prevented from driving on to the platform, and we waded the last bit.

Here we found the first snag - a Mongolian family had taken over our compartment, our booked seats. As an independent traveller by inclination, it was the first time I'd felt thankful to be "nannied"; our driver argued with the family and the *provodnik* (train attendant) and finally got us our compartment back. We found out why the family had been so loath to leave; smuggling between Russia and Mongolia is now commonplace, and they had the place crammed, from top to bottom with...shampoo. Really, I've never seen so much shampoo in my life; they had it in every nook and cranny, and kept coming back to move more of the stuff. I never did find out if it made their fortune or not.

The one day and two nights to Ulan Bator in Mongolia were far more interesting than the earlier trip, with the train going right by Lake Baikal (in mist - sod's law), and then across the sort of wide, open steppe country we'd expected to see much earlier. In Mongolia we saw our first *gers* - white rounded wood and felt homes which the nomads use. Ulan Bator was a city of *gers* until the 1940s; now it still has many on the outskirts, but the centre is a mass of depressing communist-style blocks of flats. These look OK, somehow, in Russia, but feel all wrong in Mongolia. I tried hard to like Ulan Bator, but failed, despite friendly vibrant people and wonderful Buddhist temples.

Our next event was a jeep trek into the Bayan-Gobi (where steppe and Gobi meet) to stay in a *ger* with a herdsman's family and visit Erdene Zuu, Mongolia's oldest Buddhist monastery. We had expected this to be the highlight of the trip, and it was. We rode horses with uncomfortable Mongolian saddles, milked goats, took innumerable photos. Our guide spoke excellent English, enabling us to have some interesting conversations with our hosts, in between their almost non-stop work. But then, that is the lot of farmers in Wales too. Jane presented the herdsman's children with three boomerangs acquired from the circus in Irkutsk, and they loved them. So if you should, in the future, hear a rural legend of how boomerangs were brought to Mongolia by two Western female explorers...

·

Colours of the East
Margaret Hughes (1995)

1) Hong Kong

We went in the back - a dark covered alleyway like a market - with stalls bright with red and gold, gleaming plaques and pictures, old cardboard boxes with bundles of incense sticks, signs in yellow with bold red Chinese lettering, wind chimes in red and gold with long red tassels, bottles of rice wine and smiling Chinese sales girls entreating you to come and see, come and buy. There were more booths further on - a mature businesslike man sat in each, in a Western suit but with a Chinese face. Come in, come in, they welcomed as we wandered past, come in and have your fortune told.

Round the corner, a sudden explosion of sight and sound. Torrential rain, a large courtyard - bright after the dark alley - open to the sky, bright and grey, rain bucketing down, glistening and reflecting on the tiled floor. On all four sides were covered walkways. Red pillars with gold Chinese lettering supported a bright green façade and a yellow roof, sloped and curved in the Chinese fashion, then on top another green façade and another yellow sloping roof, with carved figures of animals on the ridges and edges, like gargoyles - but exotic gargoyles. The side we had entered from had a tiny shrine, looking like a child's Wendy house. Bright red bricks were painted on each side, all no higher than a few feet, child-like. In front were a red metal table and a large golden urn.

We stood transfixed in the shelter of the walkway. To the left was the main temple building. Another long red metal table was set out with urns, lamps, baskets. Four stone tiled steps up to a brightly painted balustrade and on through the red pillars to the dark mysterious interior. Over the entrance was a large red notice, a gold and green border and large gold Chinese letters. The roof façade was green with patterns picked out in red and gold, all looking very new and clean. The yellow-tiled, double-tiered roof curved exotically.

There were people, noiseless under the sound of the rain, worshippers, standing like us in the shelter, all smaller in stature, height and breadth than us Westerners, making us feel a bit outside, different, which we surely were. But they were all intent on their business. We felt accepted, welcome to look on and see every aspect of their worship, a strange sensation for us who feel outsiders in our own churches when we go just as sightseers.

The worshippers were scuttling quickly, in their flip flop shoes, over the wet slippery tiles from shelter to shelter holding umbrellas in one hand and a bundle of incense sticks in the other. The sticks were lit at the lamps on the table, taken into the temple to be offered - to whom? Was this ancestor worship, tokens to *Feng Shui*? Having knelt and prayed, moving the smouldering sticks up and down between touching palms, the worshippers returned to place them in the huge sand-filled urns, a few in this one and tripping on to the next, a few in there. Were they placed on all sides to appease all the gods and natural forces?

We wandered slowly - the walkway opposite the entrance to the temple was crowded. Chinese people of all ages, from teenagers to very elderly great-grandparents, and in all sorts of dress from the simple Chinese silk shirts to Western blue jeans and T-shirts, they stood, sat or knelt on the floor. In front of them were offerings - a mat or even a newspaper - spread with a plate with half an oven-ready chicken, some vegetables, cakes open in a plastic bag - and little red plastic cups of wine.

Praying and bowing would be performed, completely individually with no regard for us onlookers or the other worshippers. Then the wine would be tipped from the cups onto the wet tiles, the smell of alcohol and incense making a heady perfume, another bow and the food would be quickly rewrapped in the plastic bags, the owners would be up and off, busily bustling to their next business.

The fourth and final side was less crowded. A group of young people in blue jeans and red shirts had a wooden pot half full of sticks - ah, this we had read about. Completely oblivious to us, one young man was intent on shaking the pot, the sticks rattled and sorted themselves. Slowly, one rose above the others and was quickly picked out by one of his companions. Then suddenly they were off, running over the wetness, through the rain, down to the fortune tellers at the back of the temple, to have the message on the stick interpreted, to combine the indications of this age-old way of life with their modern lives in the Chinese way.

Temple, Hong Kong, in the rain (photo: Margaret Hughes)

2) Lombok, Indonesia

We had travelled nearly halfway round the world to Indonesia and were snorkelling off Lombok, the small island next to Bali. The different scenes below the water were stunning; the coral we had travelled so far to see, so beautiful and so peaceful with the fish gliding in and out between the different colours of the reef.

A little blue fish - so tiny, so vivid, a real bright blue, brighter than any colour paint or ink we had ever seen - dark, shining eyes and a translucent tail, perfectly formed, waving slowly in the current.

We were privileged to see it, floating to just feet below us, the coral in purples, blues, greens, ivory, fish gliding between the coral fingers, darting in and out of the crevices, but none as stunningly beautiful as the tiny brilliant blue one. Perhaps it was because it was just a single specimen, alone, that attracted us. We both stopped, enthralled, and gazed at the scene.

Suddenly - a quick spurt of sand, a movement beneath us and the blue wonder disappeared. We shook our heads, looked more closely. No, it wasn't gone - a snakelike fish, barely three inches long, fat with bulging eyes, green and grey camouflage with wide jaws clamped together had a bright blue fringe around its mouth - our blue fish. Time stopped, the predator was motionless. Should we interfere?

The urge to prise open those jaws and release the blue marvel to astound other swimmers another day was strong, but we couldn't move. It was just too sudden, too awful to contemplate. Slowly, as we watched, the jaws moved and the blue fringe disappeared inside. Then, as suddenly as it had appeared, it was off. With a flick of its tail, the captor had gone - leaving us saddened, staring at a blank stretch of coral sand.

Dicing with Death
Ken Gambier (1998)

We quickly found out that the driver could speak only a little English and it was not possible to have more than a very simple conversation with him. There is only one law of road travel in India, that of the biggest taking precedence. Everyone travelling uses the same bit of road, including pedestrians. There are few usable footpaths so people walk in the road too. There are pedestrian crossings in the main towns, but no vehicle pays any attention to them. Pedestrians are held in the lowest regard and women carrying heavy loads on their heads or men herding goats in their own villages were hooted at to get out of the way of our car. We were quite ashamed at the selfishness being shown on our behalf by our driver but felt unable to express our feelings to him.

All drivers are aggressive and sound their horns at the slightest or no provocation. Large vehicles such as buses and lorries have a message at the back "please sound horn". This is because their drivers are far too busy looking at the chaos ahead of them to watch their rear mirrors to see who is overtaking. Throughout the constant hooting we did not observe any fist-waving or shouting of insults.

Indians drive on the left, a legacy of British rule. In heavy traffic every bit of the road is used regardless of which side the traffic ought to be. At level crossings, vehicles fill the road on each side of the barrier so that, when it is lifted, there is an immediate traffic jam with nobody willing to give way. On many minor roads the surface is generally so bad that everyone drives down the middle, swerving to the left (only just) in time to avoid a head-on collision. This frequently left us bouncing around on the bumpy verge before swerving back onto the metalled road. In turn our driver would overtake another vehicle, perhaps a rickshaw or a camel cart, using the full width of the right-hand lane. Any "lesser grade" traffic such as scooters or bicycles coming the other way would be expected to pull off the road to let us through. Animals were generally treated with more respect. Cows of course would be given room and even dogs were afforded space wherever possible.

Perhaps the worst example of road indiscipline occurred on a rare stretch of dual carriageway between Agra and Delhi. We had just passed a sugar factory on our left when we came face to face with two tractors towing trailers loaded with sugarcane using both our lanes in the wrong direction. Because they were bigger than our car, we had to swerve out of the way. Accidents were very frequent and, though we did not actually see one occur, we saw the aftermath several times each day, on one occasion with a dead body still in a car.

When a lorry broke down, and this happened often, it would be repaired where it stood and the driver would put rocks or branches round it to demonstrate that it was not moving and to prevent other vehicles running into the back of it. There appeared to be no restrictions on parking and vehicles frequently stopped just where it suited the driver.

We saw no sign of traffic police and wondered what would have happened if we had been involved in an accident. Our driver did not have a telephone in the car and had no way of calling for help. If he had run into a herd of goats in a village or, even worse, had knocked down a child or a sacred cow, the local people might have taken it out on us. After all, he was driving on our behalf. When police were in evidence, such as in traffic control, drivers were generally well-behaved and obeyed instructions. Drivers also observed traffic lights, but rarely gave signals when changing lanes. Headlights were not turned on until the last possible moment after dark - and not at all for many rickshaws and scooters.

The World's Newest Nation
Neil Harris (2006)

There aren't too many countries in the world where a man can display his cock in public, and not fall foul (should that be fowl?) of the law. East Timor (the world's newest nation) is one. Cock fighting is the national sport, closely followed, judging by the number of children about, by sex. Children, especially under 10s, lined the roads to wave and cheer as our two 4x4s drove through both country and town. This enthusiasm, tinged with an appealing shyness, is not confined to the youngest; even teenagers and old folk join in.

Historical highlights are few and far between. There are a few remnants of Portuguese colonial rule, and various sites of massacres and atrocities, both from the Indonesian occupation and the post-pullout breakdown of law and order.

The scenery, for such a small country, is very varied. The central highlands, when cloud cover permits, are spectacular. The highest peak is Mount Ramelau (around 3,000m), best climbed in the dark to arrive at the summit for dawn. A statue of the Virgin Mary awaits, and a very cold wind; however, the view more than compensates. The day before this ascent was spent in Hatubuilico, a widely spaced village, at around 2,000m. We were lucky enough to be there for market day, an open-air affair where women sit selling produce and cheap imported goods, while the men busy themselves with the more important tasks of cock-fighting and gambling. As one would expect, there was a village idiot on hand, an elderly man who insisted on being photographed; the reward was a bear hug of gratitude.

Suai, in the southwest, is a bit forlorn, with an unfinished concrete cathedral and a small but rather interesting market. The village idiot here was an old woman who insisted on showing me a shoe catalogue; her betel-nut-stained grin would have graced a Hammer film from the sixties. Nearby there is evidence of potential wealth for Timor Leste (the preferred name) in the form of a leaking oil well. There is an ongoing dispute between the Australian and East Timorese governments about the position of the international boundary between the two countries. At present most of the offshore oil lies in Australian territorial waters, but many say this boundary, agreed when Indonesia occupied, should be further south, giving much of the benefit of oil wealth to this very poor country.

Atauro Island is visible from Dili. Although only 24km away, there is a 4km deep trench in-between, the joint between tectonic plates. The journey across to the island had to be undertaken in a pair of outrigger canoes as our hoped-for fishing boat was out of commission. The brisk trade winds ensured a choppy ride (think three hours of being doused with lukewarm water). Atauro Island avoided the worst of the civil strife that followed Indonesia's withdrawal. The inhabitants, about 8,000, have an aura of tranquillity and contentment about them. We stayed next to the beach in an Eco Lodge, this situated close to the main town of Vila. Nearby palms swayed in the constant wind, a pleasant noise to accompany sleep in huts constructed almost entirely from the by-products of the ubiquitous coconut.

East of Dili lies Baucau, a citadel inland from the coast. Here there is a distinct Portuguese feel. Our accommodation was in a nunnery! Not the most comfortable, or quietest, bed I've ever slept in, but memorable for being lulled to sleep by the haunting sound of *Amazing Grace* in Portuguese sung by novice nuns.

Climbing to the summit of Mount Alena, a short drive inland from Baucau, is not very arduous, but as I was at the rear of our small group a little worrying. I was being followed by two boys carrying machetes. These very sharp implements were being swung into passing vegetation uncomfortably close to my head as we ascended. Their interest was pure curiosity, rather than malice aforethought.

On the second evening in Baucau we were treated to a concert by the 30 girls (aged 15 to 19) of the school run by the nuns. This was perhaps the highlight of the trip; their singing, dancing and drumming had an innocent charm that is all but absent in the western world.

Los Palos lies in the flatter eastern end of the island; here cattle roam amongst poor villages. We visited a *tais* co-op (*tais* are the local woven cloth) and a co-op for soap made from coconut oil. At these our small group was the centre of attention, especially with the younger kids. Although they were wary of strangers, the power of the digital camera and its ability to break down barriers came to the fore. It dawned on me after a while that the complete lack of interest shown by some of the old folk in their image had more to do with poor eyesight than indifference.

The Golden Land
Paul Betterton (2004)

If you happen to mention to someone that you've been to Myanmar, you'll probably get one of four responses:

a) A rather interested but confused look followed by a knowing nod when you add, "you know, it used to be called Burma".

b) A completely confused look.

c) An "Oh I LOVED it there".

Or

d) A jump to attention followed by a lecture on ethical tourism.

I want to share with you my impressions of this fantastic place, and most of all the wonderful people, but I feel compelled to start with the ethical tourism question. Pro-democracy leader Aung San Suu Kyi asks us not to visit Myanmar. She argues that tourist money goes straight to the coffers of an unelected government, which denies Burmese citizens basic civil rights. Other Burmese pro-democracy activists contend that tourism is economically important and also vital to their movement for a two-way flow of information into and out of the country.

Both arguments have credit and potential visitors to Myanmar (and all such countries of course) should do their homework, examine their commitment to responsible travel carefully, make their decision and run with it. For me, if I hadn't gone I would have missed a magical month and several hundred dollars would not have been put into local people's pockets.

At the moment there are two ways to travel in Myanmar, either with a fully hosted government tour or with a pack on your back and a guidebook in your hand. On organised tours your money all goes through the government. Independent travellers on the other hand are able to stay at privately owned hotels or guesthouses, travel and eat using non-government establishments, theoretically putting their money where it has been earned. It's hard to avoid the state tourist agency completely but my travel partner and I had a good try, taking the backpack option and a four-week visa.

So what about Myanmar as a place to visit? You'll almost certainly arrive in Yangon (formerly Rangoon). It's a typical Asian capital city in that it has too many people, too much noise, too many harassing tri-shaw drivers and run-down areas of former colonial opulence. It does however boast the huge, splendid Shwedagon Paya, one of the many self-proclaimed eighth wonders of the world that seem to proliferate in Asia these days. It is the must-see of the capital. Having taken in this gold colossus surrounded by ornate *stupas*, pavilions and shrines, we swiftly moved on in search of the real golden land.

According to *Lonely Planet*, Kipling never actually took the trip from Rangoon along the "road to Mandalay". You can't hire cars in Myanmar, but it is possible to use the road by bus or private taxi. Yangon to Mandalay is a long trip, the road is unreliable and the views fairly boring and this is one occasion where most people succumb to spending their money on a government train. Once in Mandalay, you'll find it's the nation's cultural centre and the most Burmese of the large cities. The huge grounds of the old fort and moat are overlooked by the hill from which the City took its name. A walk to the top provides good exercise and panoramic views in all directions across the fertile plains to the surrounding mountains. Interesting temples are located throughout the city, notably Kuthodaw Paya, the world's "biggest book", and it took a hard couple of days to slog around them.

The eating experience in Mandalay was for us the finest in the country. Traditional teahouses will serve you up a huge variety of delicious snack foods with which you can fill your belly for about half a dollar. In the evening a traditional local curry house will serve you a bowl of curry, bucket of rice, plate of beans, sweet corn and tomato salads, soup, all sorts of inedible fish parts, plenty of green stuff and gallons of tea for around a dollar.

From Mandalay it is possible to take several side trips to towns such as Kalaw and Hsipaw where the countryside is lush and unspoilt, and first-class hiking tours abound. Here you are near the tourist border, where large tracts of the country closed to non-nationals. You'll start feeling a bit closer to the politics and people in these areas are happier than those in the cities to talk about the government if that's your thing. People seemed to be giving out the message that the country is effectively being annexed by China; that it is "buying everything". We witnessed things that seemed to support these claims. The number of lorries heading north towards the border laden with rice, coal and teak was almost matched by the number heading south full of electrical goods that the average citizen on a monthly wage of $7 could never afford. Having said all that we didn't see any absolute poverty, and I found the Burmese people the friendliest and seemingly among the happiest I have met in around fifty countries.

Moving west from Mandalay via a gentle cruise down the scenic Ayeyarwady River, we arrived in the Bagan Archaeological Zone, my personal highlight of Myanmar. It is a valley of 4,000 temples and *stupas* in the middle of cereal fields and lush, strong trees, a reminder that this is a deeply Buddhist country. The oldest of the monuments is estimated to date back to the mid-9th century. For many people this site rivals Angkor in Cambodia and, although on a slightly smaller scale, I can't really argue with that. It is certainly easier to get around, quite magical to wander through the valley for a few days on bicycles or on the back of a horse cart. As more tourism starts to come to Myanmar, this majestic landscape is already struggling to cope. Upper floors of some of the larger temples are already closed due to the increased number of visitors, wear and tear, and safety. The message is to get there soon if you enjoy seeing such ancient sites in pristine condition.

Running out of time we had to "rush" by private taxi ($50 for ten hours and a stop at Mount Popa on the way) to the Eastern side of the country and our last stop on the standard tourist circuit, Inle Lake. Inle is famous for floating villages, floating markets and floating gardens. A one-day boat tour does the lake and everything that floats, but several more days can easily be spent walking or cycling through stunning unspoilt countryside to monasteries and hill tribes that rarely get visited. For us four weeks had flown by and it was time to return to Yangon and our flight to Bangkok.

Myanmar isn't a beach holiday destination, though it does have some, and its infrastructure is still developing. Take plenty of cash with you into the country because, like the Internet, cash points aren't allowed just yet. We stayed in decent private guesthouses and hotels; like most of this region accommodation is charged per room, so travelling with a partner is good for the budget. Breakfast is always provided, which is great if you love eggs. There weren't many souvenirs to buy unless you are a connoisseur of carved sandalwood or marionettes. On the plus side, it can be an incredibly cheap country to tour. We lived, ate well, took in shows, replenished our clothes after several months on the road, hired bicycles, took tours and travelled around the country for four weeks on just £10 each per day. Our available budget was much higher than this; we just didn't need it.

I loved this country and it's one of those places that live long in the memory. The ever-smiling people were filled with an inner peace despite all the political goings-on in their country. Particularly in the North, we found people often very politely approaching us asking to walk and talk to practise their English. And that's all they want! They don't want you to visit their carpet shop, to change your money or show you the cheapest market in town: they just want to talk. They'd walk for half an hour in the opposite direction to the way they were originally going and then thank you profusely. It was as refreshing for an Asian country as the almost complete absence of begging.

We met a student at a remote town where a bus stops for 15 minutes each day at five in the morning. At first we couldn't work out why he was so happy to see us, but in the course of the 15 minutes it transpired that, every morning, he cycles five miles to meet the bus, simply in the hope of foreigners being on board with whom he can practise his English. Every morning he carries a pot of tea, which he delighted in sharing with us. People wave and smile constantly; at Inle Lake, children ran from a field and gave us flowers as we passed by. It is so rare in the modern world to find people so genuinely friendly, curious and eager to learn. But then I suppose that's the thing; today's Burmese are still living in a world of 100 years ago.

Shwedagon Pagoda, Myanmar (photo: Paul Betterton)

Diwali Drugs Bust
Anne Rothwell (2004)

I walked through the Delhi back street café and went upstairs to our room, relieved to escape the teeming humanity. I'd seen an elephant pass the front of the café amongst the people, dogs, cows, cycle rickshaws and occasional monkey. But, this being Diwali, the festival of light, the excitement of the previous night had surpassed today's display. The street had been full of lights and the loudspeaker beside our window emitted a deafening blare of Indian music. Then a procession came by - fascinating brightly lit floats bearing Hindu deities were drawn by garlanded oxen and bands vied with the speakers in a startling cacophony. It was all so loud, so gaudy, so Indian!

However, this morning my other half Marven had ended up on a hospital drip, suffering from dehydration, but he was now resting on the bed and feeling much better. I went into the bathroom for a cooling shower. Our en-suite had a very wet floor from the leaky plumbing, a bucket in the corner in which I washed our clothes and echoing sound effects from the hawking as next door's resident performed his ablutions. There was no hot water of course, but who needed it when the cold was so refreshing and revitalising.

Returning to the bedroom draped in a bath towel, I heard a knock at the door and two men entered. It was our doctor from this morning, together with a friend who'd given him a lift on his motorbike. Unasked, he'd been concerned enough to come and check on Marven's health, even though he couldn't afford a car. His brother was a doctor in Canada and wealthy, he told us, but he felt his vocation was to stay in India, where there was so much need. They sat down and, after he'd produced a little packet containing rehydrating powder, we had a pleasant chat, even exchanging addresses. Suddenly the door burst open and there stood our landlord with two stern soldiers. They snatched up the packet of powder, sniffed it and proceeded to harangue our doctor in rapid Hindi. Eventually he persuaded them that all was genuine, he was not a drug dealer and they eventually left, foiled and no doubt disappointed.

In England, I could never imagine being crammed into a bedroom with six men and wearing nothing but a towel. Surreal!

*A Pakistani wedding, with bride and groom flanked by two bridesmaids
(photo: Helen Matthews)*

Gang Aft A-Gley
Neil Matthews (2000)

It all started last year with an e-mail from Zerina, a friend of my wife Helen from their schooldays. Zerina was getting married.

She had somehow managed to avoid an arranged marriage until now. In this case, a friend of a friend had made the introductions and Zerina and Tanvir had met for a formal engagement ceremony earlier in 1999. Zerina's fiancé and his family had allegedly thought that she seemed "a nice, simple girl". Zerina is a PhD, a research chemist, an expert in karate and a former member of the Territorial Army. In subsequent conversations with Zerina, it emerged that her husband to be was not necessarily aware of all her hobbies…

Zerina and her family were kind enough to invite us to her wedding in March 2000 in Gujrãnwãla, a town some way north of Lahore. We would be staying with the family (parents, three brothers and three sisters including Zerina) in their new house and Helen would be one of the bridesmaids. The others were another Helen, a friend of Zerina's from karate classes; Adriana, a Brazilian (and another karate colleague of Zerina) living in Britain with her boyfriend Ken; and Parissa from Iran. We also heard that Melanie, another bridesmaid, had been unable to get a flight at all and missed the wedding.

Our flight, by PIA, went better than we could have hoped. The luggage took some time to arrive from the plane, but at least it did arrive. Zerina, who had flown out by Gulf Air, told us that eight suitcases belonging to her and her family were stuck in Bahrain and unlikely to arrive until Thursday, the day after the wedding. Gulf Air were subsequently slow and uncooperative in forwarding them. Several of the group had extreme difficulty in re-arranging return flights with Gulf Air after discovering that the flight on which they had been booked did not exist. The suitcases belonging to Zerina contained clothing and other items for the wedding, including a hand-painted teapot (£2.99 from Woolworths) whose absence particularly irked her. Over the coming week, the teapot assumed almost mythical proportions, as only one other of our party had ever seen it. The phrase "it's in the suitcase / in Bahrain", as an answer to numerous queries about the location of various items, became one of the catchphrases of our stay. Zerina's youngest sister, Najma, who had flown out to

Pakistan four months earlier to make preparations, was upset to learn that her long-awaited supplies of chocolate were also detained in Bahrain.

After a two-hour minibus journey from the airport, enlivened by the sight of donkey carts, rickshaws and long-eared sheep (one of which was on the back of a moped - unwillingly), we finally reached Gujrãnwãla and the house of the Shafi family. By Pakistani standards, it was large, containing something like ten separate rooms. This would be the setting for the second day of the wedding, the most important. We did get our own large room but, to balance this, the bathroom which we were to use (shower only, no bath) was on the outside balcony and had a rudimentary bolt and no light on the first night. If the door was open, it was safe to enter. Singing in the shower seemed to be the best way to allay any confusion, and no embarrassing incidents occurred as far as I know.

Wedding, day 1: *mendi* night

After a quiet Sunday of rest and recuperation, there was a hair-raising trip on a motor rickshaw on the Monday. Pakistanis drive on the empty side of the road and use their horns instead of indicators. I might add that this gave me some insight into Zerina's driving style back in Britain - much more dangerous than any karate or TA activity.

The drive took us to the local bazaar to buy shoes, jewellery and bangles for the ladies and to collect yet more of the saris and other outfits. Bikes, mopeds, singers, beggars, drinks waiters, policemen, shoe shiners, traders and shoppers all crowded impossibly into the narrow streets.

The shoe shop was interesting: shoes came down through a hole in the ceiling for the customer to try. I had to wait outside while this went on. We were offered bottled soft drinks, with straws, at two of the shops, leading me to conclude that this was as close as you could get to a pub crawl in Pakistan.

Although Ken had opted to wear local dress for the wedding, I had chosen to keep to smart Western attire. This was a challenge, as my preferred holiday look is normally on the scruffy side of comfortable. The ladies, in their Eastern chemises and scarves, were the objects of some staring from locals, and so was I.

That evening saw simultaneous ceremonies for the bride and groom at their respective family homes. The first event was the showing of the trousseau / gifts for the groom and his family. Zerina was dressed in a bright yellow outfit, the tradition being for the bride to look fairly awful on this evening and therefore all the more beautiful the following day. Various relatives and friends prepared plates of what looked like mud pies (actually henna), sticking lit candles in the middle of each plate. Some dancing with sticks took place, uncannily like morris dancing. The bride then came down the staircase, escorted by her bridesmaids who held a long scarf above her head, and she sat on a sofa in the main living room area. She was fed some very sweet sweets by a sequence of people, while having rupees waved over her head and oil rubbed into her hair. Young girls then sat around the henna plates and sang a number of songs (whose Urdu lyrics were allegedly suggestive), each in their own key, accompanied by clapping and drums.

This all went on until quite late in the evening; the start had been postponed to enable one of the bridesmaids, Parissa, to return from Lahore where she had been trying to reconfirm her return flight. The henna ceremonies were recorded on video by a cameraman hired for the occasion (another video cameraman had been hired by the groom's family and would appear the next day). At one point, he tried to take a shot with the lens cap still on. Later, walking backwards, he almost tripped over a carpet. In the meantime, Ken was doing a much better job using the family's hand-held camcorder...

Later still, the bride and some of the bridesmaids had henna decorations set into their hands. They would not be able to wash their hands until the following morning, to enable the henna to set. So the stage was set for Tuesday...

Wedding, day 2: the big day

It is one of the quirks of Pakistani weddings that it is illegal for the bride's family to provide catering for the groom's family and guests on this day - when the ceremony is taking place in the bride's home. To get round this, Zerina's family ordered the local equivalent of packed lunches and sent them to the groom's party to eat en route.

Zerina's plan for the ceremony had been for the bridal procession to go down the main staircase and for the bride to sit on the sofa in the main living room. The groom would then follow and sit beside her. Unfortunately, her father did not agree. For reasons I never fully understood, he decreed that the bridal procession should go across the floor of the downstairs living room, from one small room to another, where the sofa would be situated - a distance of fifteen to twenty feet. The groom would then come down the staircase to join her. In order to accommodate more people upstairs, we shifted the furniture and everyone's luggage out of two of the upstairs bedrooms into the third, the room in which we would also change. Sounds simple, doesn't it?

For the rest of the morning, we helped to decorate the ceremonial room with roses and balloons. The end result looked quite effective, despite many of the intended decorations being - wait for it - in Bahrain.

At the start of the day, we were expecting the groom's party to arrive at 1pm. During the morning, we were told that this would now be 4pm. So, when they did arrive - at 3pm - nobody was ready. The bridesmaids dashed downstairs, without their jewellery on, in order to throw rose petals in welcome. They then retreated upstairs to finish dressing, while the groom and entourage also went upstairs to the main landing for the groom to sign the marriage contract. Tanvir was, to all appearances, the archetype of an Eastern prince whom you might expect to see in a film; moustachioed and handsome in his *moghul* outfit, topped by a turban which must have put his height at near seven foot. While the men sat in the main landing area, the women sat separately in bedrooms being used as overflow.

We now began a slow and nervy descent into near-farce. Once they were ready, the bridesmaids sneaked downstairs past the groom's party into the room where Zerina was being prepared - only to discover that she was already married, as she had now signed the contract. The electricity had failed earlier, making it hard for the video cameramen to do their stuff. It was also extremely hard to clear a path between the two downstairs rooms, through a number of villagers who had been gathering at the house over the past two days, and to keep guests out of the way. There were some heated discussions between the two families about exactly what was the correct sequence to follow next. The bride and bridesmaids were given a succession of conflicting stop-go instructions.

The lack of action continued until almost twilight - by which time the video men were complaining that there was not enough light for their filming and so the procession should not proceed. Eventually, the groom's family, becoming increasingly impatient and dissatisfied, brought the groom downstairs without waiting for the bridal procession, which then took place.

The small room, with the bride and groom on the sofa, now became a scrum of photographers, friends and relatives all crowding around for a view of the couple. A beggar managed to creep into the room at one point. With the video lights and a large number of cameras clicking and flashing away for what seemed like an eternity, it became a hot and tense environment. Yet more feeding of sweets to the bride ensued, along with photographs of endless permutations of people joining the couple on or behind the sofa and giving gifts or money.

Finally, the bride and groom drove off in a white limousine to the groom's family home in Lahore for the night, taking Parissa with them (it is an Islamic tradition that a female companion accompanies the bride). There were some tears from Zerina, another tradition, although they were all too genuine: she had had a long and trying day. I wasn't sure whether to feel pleased or sorry for her by this point. Amongst other things, it is a convention that the bride should spend the ceremony looking quiet and demure. This must have been an effort as Zerina is one of the last people to whom those adjectives could apply.

All in all, what with the delays, confusion, loss of electricity and tensions between the two families, we were all glad that the day was over.

Wedding, part 3: relax

The third stage took place in the impressive home of Tanvir's family in Lahore. In effect, it was a re-run of the previous day, only earlier in the day - starting at 1 pm. The ceremonial sofa was housed on a raised dais under a canopy in a central courtyard, with rows of chairs for the (exclusively male) audience. Women sat in overflow rooms to either side, where delicious *naan* breads stuffed with minced lamb were available later.

The groom's family had taken Zerina to a local beautician (for four hours) and she arrived some time after we did, looking radiant and happy. While waiting for the bride, we were given a tour of the house, including the bridal suite and the ceremonial chair where, on the Monday, Tanvir had been fed sweets and had oil applied to his hair.

Tanvir was now attired in a Western-style suit provided by the bride's family. He looked a lot more comfortable than the previous day in his more traditional outfit. The whole atmosphere was completely different from the previous day - altogether more relaxed. Maybe this was partly because our party arrived absolutely bang on time, hence giving the groom's family nothing to complain about.

Tanvir came up to introduce himself to me about three seconds after I had accepted a bottled soft drink. We shook hands and, after a brief pause while my brain got out of neutral, embraced in the customary greeting. I was still holding the bottle.

Ken and I were quizzed by a couple of the other guests about our children (lack of). Ken said he and Adriana had been married for a year.

"And is it the will of God that you have no children yet?"

Ken answered with some diplomacy that it was partly that, and partly his and Adriana's will, aided by suitable precautions. When our inquisitor found out that I had been married for nine years, relief stole over his face...until I confirmed that I, too, had no children and no wish for any.

Photographs of the happy couple and various others followed once more, and people came up one after another to present Tanvir with money as part of the ritual. Next to him, one of his sisters was recording each gift in a notebook. This is a pragmatic tradition, in case a divorce occurs later and the various gifts need to be returned. Another much-used phrase during the week, in answer to queries, was "It's traditional". At some points, the two families seemed to have different ideas of what constituted a tradition.

This was a more decorous and enjoyable day all round.

We left a couple of days later, after a trip to Lahore on Thursday, the purpose of our visit now complete. It had been quite a week. Virtually no activity happened as planned or on time. Robert Burns' line that "The best laid plans o' mice an' men / Gang aft a-gley" might have been specially written for Pakistan. But despite the problems and delays, we were privileged to be invited into a Pakistani home and to play a small part in an important day in the life of a family and a dear friend. We'll remember it always.

The Curse of Paradise
John Keeble (2003)

I spent a few days at a Thai beach resort. And it changed my lives... which was something of a surprise, given that I've been slipping away to the magic land at every opportunity since the mid-70s.

The problem was that this was no ordinary beach on Ko Samui or Ko Lanta. Nothing as universally familiar as Phuket, nothing so well trodden as James Bond Island.

No, this was...well, paradise. On Ko Phi Phi, hazing limpid greens in the Andaman Sea between Lanta and Phuket.

We arrived on the island by ferry after a couple of weeks in northern Burma, at a time when the military junta looked like finding its way towards some kind of compromise with the democracy movement, and another couple of weeks mooching around Krabi in southern Thailand.

Our boat eased on to the side of another boat lashed to the side of a jetty in a wide bay and we dragged our bags over the assorted ironwork and down to the beach where the longtail boats seemed like they might take us to Pee Pee Island Village, one of Ko Phi Phi's upmarket resorts, whose name catches the English pronunciation of Phi Phi.

It did not look like *The Beach* of Leonardo DiCaprio fame, though it should because it was the other side of the thin isthmus from the beach used in the film, not mirror images but near enough to make you not care. The tropical idyll basics were there but the developers had beaten us to it.

Not a big surprise: there have been reports for years about damage to some parts of the island and to the seabed.

But that was not where we were going. Our destination was a careful development where there were no roads and limited building. So we hired our boat, splashed into the sea to get in, and set off...

It had been 18 months since we had been in a longtail boat on the Andaman Sea: then it had been a temperamental monsoon day, one minute glistening with the hazy white gold sunlight, the next the swell of a deep green molten metal sea, and then suddenly blowing up a storm that had us racing for shelter by one of the hundreds of karst islands in Phang Nga bay.

On the day we arrived at Phi Phi, the sun was high in the early afternoon, the sea flowing blues and greens that threatened nothing to upset the stillness and the only noise was the beat of the engine as we chugged past the coves, round the tiny headlands.

In fact, it was all very ordinary at that point and no hint of the problem ahead.

Perhaps the first indication, looking back with 20/20 hindsight, was when the Pee Pee Island Village Resort came into view a few hundred yards into a generous bay rimmed with yellow-white sand and backed by jungled hills.

The boat slid into the rising seabed and stopped, grounded, before it could reach the gentle foam where water lapped hopefully at the shore. We went over the side, Phi Phi style, and waded ashore.

A tall young Thai reached into the boat and lifted out our bags, lugging them up the beach and into the wooden reception. June, my wife, remarked (somewhat breathlessly, I thought) how strong he was and I concurred, having lugged the same bags myself. We have - *had*, I should write now - a system where June packed and I carried. It doesn't work.

Anyway, the reception staff, in their Thai traditional best, greeted us, gave us damp perfumed towels to rid ourselves of the journey's residues, and cooling coconut cocktails. So far, so good.

Then the strong young lad wheeled off our bags towards our chalet in the jungle of carefully tended flowers, trees and other chalets. We followed. It was then that the disastrous chain of events began in earnest.

June walked on but, as we rounded a bend on the path by the beach, I hesitated, looking between the palm trees into the shimmering green-blue vapour blending sea and sky, barely different as they stretched off to the tranquil grey silhouette of a small island a mile or two off shore.

I lifted my camera, clicked off a couple almost automatically for my mind and my senses were being sucked into the place and I realised that this, after traipsing the world for three decades, was it. Paradise. Though, even then, I didn't realise what that would ultimately mean.

As we walked on, with an occasional glance back, the resort unfolded over the acres between the beach and the valley areas behind, with their tracks and the islanders' village straggling along the tidal river and mangroves. Ahead of us were the spinal hills with steep, then unseen, jungle paths to other bays.

Forgive the detail. It's too much, I know. But it is important to understanding what was fast approaching.

I rarely crave luxury but enjoy it when it is there, like the time when we had a few days up near Khao Lak on Thailand's Andaman coast after being drained of blood by the hungry leeches of Khao Sok jungle park - or, down in southern Laos, staying for a couple of days in a converted palace. Our chalet, at a princely Thai sum of around £60 a night, had a large bedroom, satellite TV, a dressing room, wash area and shower room and a generous verandah. And someone slipping in unseen to turn down the bed and romantically lay a fresh flower on it. At the entrance, a large earthenware jar was filled with water and, each morning before we awoke, the surface of the water was redecorated with petals.

There was something fascinating about the flower art, not just the colours and the patterns but also the tranquillity of it, the serenity of its creations before most guests stirred in time for breakfast. The theming, too, built on it with small decorations by guests' chalets, large designs by the breakfast restaurant and the huge reception displays, the biggest taking two women at a time to prepare it before guests started their days.

That first evening, we ate in the main restaurant. Open-air, a tropical fragrance running through the night air, and the ever-helpful Thais bending their long menu into vegan shapes to please us. Lemon grass and kaffir lime leaves, coriander and chillies, coconut and subtle curries, rich fruits...Singha beer, an old friend, chilled like champagne.

Afterwards, we lay on loungers away from the lights. Just watching the stars parade across the black sky and listening to the gentle tide. Not far away, a notice proclaimed in daylight hours: Beware of falling coconuts. We always take that seriously after a huge coconut fell 50ft and missed by inches nutting June as we strolled on Ko Samui some years ago. But then, on Phi Phi, nothing fell... except us, perhaps, under the island's spell.

The next day, looking back now, seems to be summed up in an image: or, rather, if one image sums up the day it was the perfect shadow of the palm tree considerately spreading itself across the fine sand for our convenience as we lazed a little, swam a little, then sat by the bar behind the beach while cheerful young men prepared exotic drinks and biked over to the kitchens for vegetable spring rolls for our lunchtime snack.

The evening brought a new experience. As the sun went down, over a deep bay naked without its covering tide, the wonders of people and nature competed for the heart, the mind and the spirit. We walked on sand over which we had swum in the day, surveying a scene - many micro-scenes - of natural beauty and quiet human purposefulness. As a backdrop, the dusk sky was changing colour through the blues, yellows and oranges to every possibility of mauve and finally greys.

Suddenly the air was rent with the sound of an engine and an old tractor trundled out to the water's edge where a longtail boat was stranded, like a sleek whale, on the sand and half a dozen people were looking hopeful of a ride somewhere. The tractor hooked on the boat and dragged it into the sea, its vertical exhaust clear of the water slopping over the machine and driver, and the boat's passengers climbed in for their journey to... who knows where?

Away to the left, the sun was lighting up islands and clouds were rearranging themselves, jockeying for a good position for our lenses as the light changed and the sun slipped away. On the edge of the water, in front of the sea stretching to the islands, a young couple formed evocative shapes as she posed for him to photograph her. A late returning longtail chugged in, stopped short of grounding in the channel to the village, and a woman got out and waded easily, comfortably, towards her home.

On the third day, we arose early, eager but now wondering if the worst could, after all, be true. There were no other guests around, just us and the staff who worked quietly like the secret crews of Westworld to return the resort to its perfect state. Paths and facilities were swept, supplies sorted, restaurants prepared...and, what we were seeking, the flower art was emerging after the women had collected their materials petal by petal at the first hint of dawn. They smiled, welcomed us as we photographed, several rolls of transparencies and still more with the digital. Scenes, close-ups, this design, that...

Then we ate breakfast in the buffet restaurant, open to the sea views but much with shade from the advancing sun. There was a culinary choice spanning Asia, Europe and America, a mix and match that seemed endless. Wild birds - well, not so wild, really - fluttered down to share what we gave them.

We had a bit of a plan, as much as we ever make, for a day of walking. Not another day on the beach; we had done enough of that the day before, but a walk of exploration. Through the resort, through the

Talking on the beach (photo: June Keeble)

locals' territory with its evidence of life behind the manicured front, and on to a jungle path over the hill towards another bay.

One of the endlessly pleasant aspects of South East Asia is how quickly you can find yourself in the wild, the protection of anything Western gone and the local way the only way. That was how the paths were: so steep at times that they needed ropes and old electrical wire to help the walker up or down, the trees hanging across them, the occasional worker struggling to cut bamboo on their edges...and the sudden, startlingly beautiful views of bays springing from the wall of greenery without warning.

When we got back, we had a cocktail in a bar tucked away behind the beach and trudged back to our chalet for a shower, a rest and another go at the restaurant's addictive menu.

The next day was our last on Phi Phi. A longtail boat out to a sea rendezvous with the Phuket ferry, a ride to the country's most popular island...and the flight home without having to check in at Bangkok. As we contemplated that, I had to admit...I was ready to go. And that is where the real problem inescapably condensed to question the whole basis of my eternal intentions.

For here I was in paradise, with normal people proclaiming they would never leave it, and I was bored. Not horribly bored. Just on the edge of boredom that would get worse if I stayed on day four and become intolerable on day five. Worse, it was a Thai paradise. A Thai beach paradise.

Some people see death as final. They live their life out with that expectation. And they might be right. Who knows? But I rather like the Buddhist view: endless lives of misery until I stop lusting after...well, you know, the usual things.

So I have this arrangement with June. I'll take my male prerogative to slip away quietly into the next world a little earlier than her, wait for a few decades - her time here and all that next-world yakking as she catches up with her pals - on a Thai beach. She comes to find me and we work out what we want to do in the next incarnation.

Now, tragically, all that is out of the cosmic window. If I get bored in just a few days in paradise, how can it work?

But perhaps next winter I'll pop back to paradise, just to make sure...

Birdman and Other Legends
Wendy May (2002)

The isolation of Easter Island is difficult to comprehend from maps. It is 2,300 miles west of South America and 2,515 miles to the east of Tahiti. It was only on the five-hour flight from Santiago that it began to dawn on me how isolated the island really is. The first surprise was the long time it took to taxi along the runway. We later discovered that the runway had been significantly extended to enable an emergency landing of the space shuttle!

I was not really expecting the masses of people at midnight, when our flight arrived. We entered the small baggage hall to collect our cases and were greeted with a row of booths where islanders were sitting offering bed and breakfast accommodation. Outside there were crowds of people welcoming arrivals and giving us flower garlands.

I was expecting a barren island - no trees, very windy and very dusty. It was actually hot and humid with a sound of crickets chirruping in the background. The main village is Hanga Roa (population 3,000) and every house seems to have a vegetable garden, banana and citrus trees and flowers including hibiscus and bougainvillea. There are also avocado and papaya trees, with pineapple, guava and watermelon. The vegetation does not reflect that of earlier times: originally there were forests of palm, conifers and hardwoods; now, thanks to a reforestation programme, there are groves of eucalyptus trees. There are very few bird species. Sparrow hawks were introduced into the island and they seem to have proliferated at the expense of the other birds and on one journey across the island I saw a line of about twenty birds perched on the posts of a boundary fence.

As we travelled along the red, dusty roads to explore the island - only the main streets in Hanga Roa are paved - it became obvious that it would be very easy to miss things if travelling without a local guide. The volcanic south coast is very beautiful and it would be easy to overlook the piles of rocks along the coastline. Many of these are actually ancient *ahu*, with fallen *moai*. In fact there are almost 350 *ahu* around the coast, sited in sheltered coves and in areas favourable for human habitation.

The *ahu* is the religious shrine for a community - and also the burial or cremation site. They face inland towards the community and most of them have a well constructed sea wall to the rear. One of the sites, at Vinapu, has a sea wall built in the Inca style - which led Thor Heyerdahl to develop his theory that the original inhabitants of the island came from South America. In front of some of the *ahu* there is a circle of rocks - the death circle - where bodies were laid (after being washed, disembowelled and wrapped in a bark cloth) for three days prior to burial or cremation.

The *moai* are thought to represent the elders of the community. On their death the *moai* - a stylised image representing the individual - is erected on the *ahu*. It faces inland towards the community to give it his knowledge, protection and strength. All the *moai* appear to be male and were carved from tuff - a volcanic stone from the crater of Ranu Raraku. Most are weathered and covered with a white lichen. These fallen *moai* looked very sad - most laying face downwards among the stones of the *ahu*. They reminded me of fallen gravestones in an old village churchyard.

Scattered around the *ahu* there are also cylinders of red rock (*scoria*) known as top knots (*pukao*) and which sat on top of the *moai*, representing their hair. Apparently the men used to dye their hair with crushed *scoria* mixed with sugar-cane juice to give a red colour (a bit like henna). It was interesting to note that the male islanders still wear their hair long and occasionally wear it tied up into a topknot.

There are a number of *ahu* sites and *moai* which have been restored over the last 30 years and it is these that provide some of the main images from Easter Island. However, for me, the most exciting part of the visit was the quarry at Ranu Raraku - where all the *moai* had been carved. There are hundreds of unfinished *moai* on the slopes, most of which are buried up to their shoulders or necks in the earth so that only their heads are visible. These are eye-less *moai* as the eye sockets were only completed when the *moai* had been raised onto its designated *ahu*. There is also one *moai* which has legs - this is Tukuturi (the kneeling *moai*), one of the few *moai* that actually has a name. The stylised *moai* faces are thin and angular, with long noses and ears, and have a disdainful look.

As there was no source of metal on the island all the *moai* had been carved out from the rock using obsidian and basalt tools, making the most of fault lines in the rock. The *moai* were carved in situ and there are still unfinished *moai* attached to the quarry face, including the largest *moai* ever carved - 'El Gigante' - which is 20 metres long. When a *moai* had been detached from the rock it was raised into a standing position in a trench so that it could be finished. It is these unfinished *moai* standing in their trenches, now covered in earth, that form the heads. (It is estimated that two teams, working in shifts, could carve a medium-sized *moai* in 12-15 months. This work must have involved considerable team work and manpower.)

From the quarry we could see the 15 standing *moai* on *ahu* Tongariki on the coast. As we got closer to the site it was possible to see that although the *moai* have a stylised form all these *moai* were different, representing different faces and individuals. They also clearly showed the stylised form of the *moai* body - a protruding stomach (to give a low centre of gravity), an arched back, pronounced nipples, a belly button, arms, hands and long fingers.

While Tongariki was the largest *ahu* we visited the other restored sites were no less majestic. Anakena on the north coast has a beautiful beach, with golden sand, surrounded by palm trees. This is a special place for the islanders as it is thought to be the landing site of Hotu Matu'a, the island's first coloniser. It is also where the locals come to spend a relaxing afternoon. The *moai* of *ahu* Nau Nau located here had been buried in sand and so are not as weathered as other *maoi* and they show spiral designs on their backs - which are thought to represent tattoos. Although many photographs and postcards show the these *moai* with eyes they are now eye-less and the single remaining eye on the island (made from coral) is in the museum. Also here is the sole *moai* of *ahu* Ature Huki - the first *moai* to be re-erected on the island.

There is one *moai* on the island which has been given eyes - this is the *moai* on *ahu* Kote Riku - and which is known as the 'one who looks to the sky'. This *moai* is found at Tahai, an *ahu* complex just outside the town of Hanga Roa. The earliest site here dates back to the sixth century AD. There are three *ahu* here, the first with the remains of five standing *moai*, and two with a single *moai*. This site seems to have been a major ceremonial area and there are also the remains of houses (which looked like upturned canoes and are called boat houses), caves, chicken houses and a harbour.

Probably the most intriguing site is *ahu* Akiva, where seven *moai* have been erected inland and which look towards the sea. The local legend is that the *moai* represent the seven men sent to the island, as a scouting party, by the first king. The *moai* are orientated to the summer solstice and may have been significant for calendar setting. The other *moai* erected inland is on *ahu* Huri a Urenga and is known as the *moai* 'that belongs to the moon'. This is a special *moai* as it has two pairs of

The one who looks to the sky (photo: Wendy May)

arms. Its 20 fingers are thought to represent the 20 constellations known to the tribes and used for navigation.

Following the *ahu/moai* period of the island's history, there appears to have been social disintegration resulting in inter-tribal warfare and destruction of the *ahu*. An intriguing result of changes to the social system after this period was the development of the birdman cult. The birdman festival took place in September, when the chiefs of the island groups gathered at Orongo - which perches on the rim of the crater of Ranu Kau, and with a cliff drop of 300 metres. From this vantage point it is possible to see in all directions - to an unending vista of empty ocean. You can also see the curvature of the earth! The festival involved a competition between the tribal groups, the aim of which was to find the first egg of the sooty tern to be laid on Motu Nui, the largest of three islets situated about 2km out to sea. The egg hunters had to scale down the cliffs, swim to Motu Nui, find the egg and return with it tucked into a headband. The chief of the victorious tribe was then crowned as birdman. It could take several weeks to find the egg and the priests and those who remained at Oronga participated in ritual dances, songs and prayers. The sacred area, where the priests lived, has a large number of petroglyphs of Makemake (the god of the island) and of the birdman, and has a spectacular view of the islets. The site here has recently been reconstructed as it was a location for the film *Rapa Nui* made by Kevin Costner.

What about modern culture? The islanders speak Rapanui although many also speak Spanish and English. The community is mainly Catholic and the church in Hanga Roa has a number of beautiful wood carvings incorporating both Catholic and birdman symbols. We attended mass on Sunday morning and most of the island appeared to be in attendance. The priest greeted everyone at the door and conducted the service in Spanish, Rapanui and English. There was no organ, but locals arrived with guitars and accordions to provide the musical accompaniment. The church has a high wooden roof and the singing and music filled the building. I can honestly say that this was an uplifting experience and one which gave a tingle factor. The warmth and friendliness of the islanders was almost palpable.

Although the islanders rely on tourism it is very low key. There are several small hotels on the island but most accommodation is in local homes. Our guide told us that there had recently been an application to build a large 5-star hotel complete with golf course and the islanders were hoping that this would be rejected. There are a few tourist shops selling local woodcarvings and stone (pumice) *moai*, as well as T-shirts, and *rongo rongo* carvings - a pictographic form of writing which has not yet been deciphered. Some enterprising islanders also set up stalls at the main sites and there is a local market in the mornings for fruit, vegetables, fish and souvenirs.

There are only two flights per week to and from mainland Chile and the islanders call into the local post office to collect and deliver mail - there are no mail deliveries. I was lucky when I visited the post office as I had my passport with me and was able to get it stamped as a record of my visit to the island. There are no newspapers on the island and the local TV station only broadcasts for a few hours each day so the islanders appear to keep up with local news through regular contact at church, in the market or at the post office.

As everything not grown locally has to be imported, certain food items can be expensive and the main diet is local fish and chicken. One local speciality is an ice cream, made from a local fruit, which has a peach-like flavour and which has lines of vanilla ice cream threaded within it (delicious). They also make a mean *pisco* sour and a sweeter alternative - *pisco* pineapple.

On leaving the island we were all given shell necklaces - so that we would have something by which to remember our stay on the island. I don't think I will forget this holiday - the isolation, the friendliness, the *moai* and drinking a *pisco* sour while watching the sunset.

Ten Days in Tibet
Helen Krasner (1997)

I had wanted to go to Tibet since I was ten years old. That was when I read Heinrich Harrer's bestseller, *Seven Years in Tibet*, in which he tells of escaping from a prison camp in India, walking across the Tibetan plateau in winter and finally being one of the first Westerners to reach Lhasa, the Forbidden City - where he eventually became friend and confidant to the young Dalai Lama. I had childishly yearned to follow in Harrer's footsteps. But times change. In the 1950s, the Chinese invaded Tibet, bringing roads and machinery and other trappings of "progress", destroying temples and monasteries and changing the age-old culture forever. In 1959, the Dalai Lama fled to India where he set up the Tibetan Government in exile. Tibet was closed to foreigners for many years and my vague plans for walking across the Himalayas to get in were hardly practical. But, since 1986, tourists have been allowed in on a limited basis and I finally scraped together the cash needed by Chinese-inflated prices for a trip to "The Roof of the World".

"Are you going trekking?" I was asked continuously when I told friends I was going to Tibet. No, I told them, it was a cultural tour. I hoped that I was right and that Tibetan culture still existed. At first, at least, I was not disappointed. On the drive to Lhasa from the airport, we stopped at a small temple, where I was surprised to see photos of the Dalai Lama on display; I believed they had been outlawed. The Tibetan tour guide shrugged. "When the police come they take them down; when they go, the monks put them back," she told us. Perhaps things were not as bad as I'd heard.

But in Lhasa? It is slowly becoming more Chinese, with wide roads, modern buildings and a huge square in front of the Potala Palace (built in 1994) epitomising the Chinese mania for hugeness and open spaces. Only the centre of Lhasa, the Barkhor, is still Tibetan. There were weird and wonderfully dressed pilgrims from all four corners of Tibet prostrating themselves in front of the Jokhang temple; stalls selling lumps of turquoise, yak fur coats, prayer wheels and carpets; and everywhere the smell of slightly rancid yak butter and a steady hum of the devout chanting "Om Mani Padme Hum" ("Hail to the Jewel in the Lotus").

Yet, even in the Barkhor, the Chinese army are everywhere in evidence, stationed every hundred yards or so, watching. I had heard that Tibetans live in fear, afraid to talk politics or fraternise with foreigners. This was confirmed by a political discussion with an English-speaking Tibetan outside the Norbulingka, the summer palace. He confirmed that Tibetans trust nobody but close family; the Chinese pay informers well and people are poor. They can be jailed for little or no reason. Nevertheless, he assured me, "I believe that ninety per cent of Tibetans have courage." When alone, they do not use the Chinese language and do what they can to keep their religion and culture alive.

But they can do painfully little. Chinese immigration increases yearly, with high salaries and bonuses promised to those Chinese who will relocate to Tibet. All education is in Chinese and jobs for Tibetans are hard to find. My conversation with this brave man - who was taking an incredible risk - ended when a van appeared. Hearing all this is a great shock, even if one has read about it.

In our few days in Lhasa we visited the Potala Palace, ransacked by the Chinese but now restored, the two largest monasteries - where the monks are now back and practising their religion - and a number of other sights. We ate Tibetan food and drank the famous butter tea - quite palatable if you think of it as soup rather than tea and, I'm sure, excellent in winter. We talked with people and bargained for trinkets and took innumerable photos, for it is an incredibly photogenic country. Then, on the fifth day, we piled on to our bus for an overland trip back to Nepal, via Gyantse and Shigatse, Tibet's other two cities.

Tibet is a land of superlatives, with the highest mountains, deepest gorges, driest climate - the list is endless. Virtually the whole of the Tibetan plateau is over 10,000 feet. Lhasa, at 12,000 feet, is in a valley, though this did not prevent mild symptoms of altitude sickness - suffered by almost all visitors. Our trip took us over a pass, down multi-coloured mountains to a huge turquoise lake, up through a number of passes of over 17,000 feet, past villages, nomad encampments and farmers with their yaks. We were on the main road, the "Friendship Highway"; it is a dirt track often blocked by rubble and landslides. Fifteen miles an hour was our best average and I was reminded that Tibet didn't even have the wheel until the Chinese came. We took photos of Everest from three different places. It was dry, dusty, exhilarating, exhausting, but never boring.

On the last day, we drove through a gorge with sheer drops into endless nothingness, where both the river below and the tops of the mountains above were almost invisible. We dropped over 10,000 feet in twelve hours from dry dusty desert to humid rainforest and our bodies and lungs protested. 150 people had died building this road. It is narrow and dangerous and frequently impassable because of landslides. It is incredible simply by being there at all.

We spent our last night in Tibet in Zhangmu, seven kilometres from the border. The town clings perilously to the side of the mountain, its roads permanent mud from the rain every afternoon. Its people are both Nepalese and Tibetan, its atmosphere felt like neither, I thought - and yet...

Next day, we crossed the Friendship Bridge to Kodari, the first village in Nepal. Kodari is a dusty collection of huts, a village whose sole *raison d'être* appears to be to serve the relatively few travellers across the border. Its people are poor, its buildings decaying and it has nothing to recommend it - except freedom. The change in atmosphere from Tibet to Nepal was almost tangible - the feeling of relaxation, the lack of fear, in a poor country which was being allowed to grow or decay at its own rate, in its own way. I felt horribly guilty about having enjoyed ten days in Tibet.

Human traffic light substitute, North Korea (photo: Neil Harris)

The World According to KIS
Neil Harris (2005)

Wherever you go in P'Yŏngyang the Ryugyong Hotel is visible, only officially it doesn't exist. It would be the highest hotel in the world; if only it had been finished. The official line is that the French architect used the wrong concrete, so it is unsafe. The truth seems to be that the money ran out. Lack of money and/or resources, along with political ideology, guide almost everything in North Korea. Kim Il Sung, known as the Great Leader and designated the Eternal President, stares down from innumerable murals and mosaics. This is the World according to KIS.

Tourism is strictly controlled. Only 1,000 non-Chinese tourists per year are allowed entry; these are in groups shepherded by two guides, to sites that show North Korea in the best possible light. Getting beneath the veneer is extremely difficult.

The people of P'Yŏngyang are well off in comparison with those elsewhere; the train journey from China through fertile coastal plains allowed a glimpse of rural poverty. Here, I suspect, was the real North Korea. P'Yŏngyang is a city built to a plan; with a little paint it could be quite handsome; but, since the fall of the Soviet Union, money has been tight and it shows. Like all Communist oligarchies, monuments are on the grand scale, and on occasion rather optimistic, such as the Re-unification Monument (under Communism of course). A pilgrimage to the huge bronze statue of Kim Il Sung is compulsory, as is a visit to his birthplace; a remarkably well-preserved farmhouse just outside P'Yŏngyang.

Next on the menu is the Demilitarised Zone, the heavily mined 4km-wide corridor between North and South. This involves a 100km drive down an empty (apart from some broken-down Chinese Landrovers) dual carriageway to Kaesong. The story according to KIS is that the US invaded North Korea and that the brave North Koreans threw the Yankee imperialist dogs out. Five huts straddle the border, the central one of which still hosts meetings to discus the terms of the armistice between the two sides; the war has technically never ended. A table sits astride the border, three chairs either side and at both ends a chair for the interpreters who sit with one leg in North Korea, the other in South Korea.

After a quick return to P'Yŏngyang, the other excursion was to Wŏnsan on the east coast. This sits on the Korean Sea (otherwise known as the Sea of Japan). Here foreigners are a rare sight. Our visit coincided with North Korean National Day and, thanks to an unscheduled repair to our coach, we were able to wander around town, still carefully shepherded by our two guides. Large floral tributes were being laid at the bronze statue of KIS by various groups of uniformed North Koreans, ranging from primary school children to People's Army Officers. We were allowed to butt in, then expected to go and bow to the Great Leader.

Back in P'Yŏngyang we spent the evening of National Day in KIS Square where 50,000 North Koreans were assembled. On the stroke of eight they started to dance *en masse*; allegedly traditional Korean folk dances. This appeared to be largely for the benefit of the audience of perhaps 200 foreigners and maybe 100 North Korean dignitaries. After about 20 minutes we were cajoled into joining in and then allowed to wander amongst the dancers. At nine the dancing stopped abruptly, the dancers dispersing at breakneck speed. I had the feeling they were there under duress. Little did we realise that, as we joined in the fun, a large mushroom cloud in the north of the country was creating an international incident.

The trip finale was a visit to the Children's Palace. This is an institute founded to show off North Korean youth at their best and also as a teaching institution of the arts and crafts. After being pushed into various classes in session, we watched the show. This takes place in a large theatre and is attended by the few tourists and many local school children. At the finale the backdrop was of the Great Leader and Dear Leader, Kim Il Jong, along with adoring children. As this appeared, the audience gave what seemed to be a loud spontaneous cheer. Perhaps you *can* fool all the people all of the time!

The Accidental Pilgrim
John Keeble (2004)

There was a moment, between the impossible behind us and the impossible ahead, when I disappeared along with the rest of the churning universe of my mind, and the pilgrimage mountain and life merged and stretched ahead, still and inevitable.

I did not know how it had happened, or even what had happened, only that I had started the eight-mile climb of Sri Pada, Sri Lanka's holy mountain, as a tourist and now, in the black stillness of the jungle night, I felt a pilgrim.

Rational logic, imported on an Airbus from London, and doubts melted into calm purposefulness while aching muscles and jarred joints eased. The lights that crowned Sri Pada still spiralled half way to the *poya* moon, with false trails snaking left and right, but it did not matter. Everything was in place, inevitable, right.

Sri Pada means Sacred Footprint, the rock indentation that Buddhists say was left by Buddha on the top of the 2,224 metre (7,360ft) peak. Muslims call it Adam's Peak and say the footprint came from Adam's first step into our world after being cast out of paradise. Hindus believe it was made by Lord Shiva. Some call the peak Samanalankande - the mountain where butterflies go to die.

But, whatever the reason, whatever the beliefs, pilgrims have been on the peak for more than a thousand years, their suffering making karmic merit in this world and the next... and their merit as people making them suffer sometimes to the point of death.

A few days before our time on the peak we had met the Venerable S. Dhammakiththi Thero, the high priest of Aukana, the site of Sri Lanka's most famous Buddha image. The 40ft standing Buddha was carved from the living rock some 1,500 years ago: today, Dhammakiththi - pronounced "Dharmakeetee" - and his close lay associates are revitalising the community with a new Buddhist purpose, a new school and a new hope for the future.

He had a charismatic presence, at once an unworldly monk and a dynamic leader, and unusually he waited for the dawn sun and our film to agree before going through the morning ritual of offering flowers and prayers to the Buddha.

That was the start of a friendship with him and his community that led us to Sri Pada on the next *poya* - full moon holiday - in the company of 20 or so people from his Aukana Rajamaha Viharaya temple complex, some of the teachers from the associated school and others from the local community.

For them, the only route was the long traditional climb from Ratnapura. The quick route, a mere six-hour climb from another direction, was better than nothing for those who could not manage the proper route and for tourists who needed experiences rather than wanting to make merit. But it was not even a consideration for our Buddhist group.

For us, too, it was not a consideration - though for different reasons. We had eaten no more than snacks for two days as we went from one experience to another - the February festival in Colombo, the Bo-Path Ella waterfall near Ratnapura - and, with more determination than physical fitness, we were just taking it all in our mental stride as part of a group that had no doubts.

Our two vans - one that collected us from Colombo and the other direct from Aukana with Dhammakiththi and the temple party - arrived at Sri Rajasinharanaya temple at Palabakhala, near Ratnapura, at the start of the pilgrimage route. Dhammakiththi, the supreme networker, had arranged with the monks for his party to be given a cool room, access to facilities and tea with jaggery.

Refreshed, we grouped off to the Buddha shrine and then to a ritual where a temple official named us to the gods and asked them to protect us on the mountain, a coin wrapped in cloth and soaked in coconut oil bound round our right wrists - coin up for men, coin down for women - to mark us out from the less devout and wary.

June, my wife, took our group photos; a stray German (the only other westerner we saw on the route) wandered into the group and was caught forever with us.

Dhammakiththi said goodbye: he was staying behind. A few years ago, before the peace between the Singalese and the Tamils, his dynamic community leadership made him a target for a Tiger bomber and he was left with damaged knees, an injured eye and a police bodyguard carrying a submachine-gun.

Our party set off around 5pm with the day cooling: a nurse and an architect with their nine-year-old and two-year-old daughters, the young temple ladies as bright and demure as a Sunday school outing, a teacher with his wife and young son, a woman with a walking stick and two girls to help her, men in their 20s to 40s, and June and me.

No one took much: just water, food and warm clothes to protect against the cold of the night on the mountain. We were the only ones wearing anything on our feet - and then only footwear we would use for a stroll in our Cambridgeshire village on a summer's afternoon. Our bags had extra water, a few clothes and, of course, our weighty cameras, lenses and film... we had no idea how much we were going to suffer for our dubious art.

At one time, pilgrims climbed the raw mountain but today the route has some concessions to the frailties of the human form. It has electric lights at intervals, tea shops where people can rest and get a variety of drinks on the trail, and the start warms up with 2,200 concrete steps which end about half way up the first of two smaller mountains that the routes crosses before it gets to Sri Pada itself.

It was a pretty walk at that stage, through tea fields with brightly dressed girls plucking the young leaves, and past the first of the tea shops that line the route. A young man, bent almost double by a huge sack of supplies for one of the higher rest stops, steadily overtook us. One of the kindly group looked back to see how we were faring: no problem.

The first intimation of the true difficulties of the climb came when Western notions of what constitues a path petered out with the concrete steps and the climb, over just the first mountain, began in earnest from boulder step to boulder step, across huge rock surfaces chiselled with shallow footholds, through streams and over rivers, by precipitous drops into the engulfing jungle.

Young men passed us, leaping ahead with the traditional chants, but our group straggled and struggled on, coalescing at times so we could all sit together on the rocks or at the tea shops perched by the trail. Some knew how far we had to go: we had an ignorance that protected us until the hours and the effort stripped away the optimism and made us wonder just what we were doing.

By the highest point crossing the second mountain, the effort was eating into our reserves, sapping our strength and our water and reducing our horizon to the next boulder, the next jarring step down some black crevice in the trail.

And the group - the very opposite of the competitive Western trekkers in Thailand's northern hills - was closing up, everyone helping everyone else: a careful eye on the children, now flagging; on the bravely struggling woman with the walking stick; on older members of the party; and on us, out of pace and place, with one of the younger men gently insisting on carrying my bag, so I could carry June's, and two others carefully offering supporting arms for June at particularly difficult places.

Finally, we reached the beginning of Sri Pada: we were on the mountain itself and the *poya* moon - so spiritually significant to the pilgrims - was rising clear and free of cloud, lighting up the trail like daylight and casting shadows as black as despair where not even the occasional pilgrim lights penetrated.

But by then, with 7,000 feet to climb, the world for us had closed in to the next 2ft upwards heave, our clothes so wet with perspiration that it felt like we had emerged from a river. Around us were the jungle sounds, the occasional voice of the others. Ideas of staying clean had vanished and now we slumped gratefully on to rocks or ledges or roots without heed for water or insects or snakes...

A few minutes later when it was time to go, one of the enthusiastic men would cry out: "Madam! Go!" And we would all grind on as far as we could: the nurse carrying her two-year-old, the woman with the stick fighting one step forward at a time, our weary Western muscles quivering and our knees threatening to give way.

At one stop Wasala, a serenely kind friend, told us: "We're late." But we could not fight through the exhaustion to care - though we might if we had known that the solicitous Dhammakiththi had got the monks at the top to cook a meal for our party, a rare treat when most pilgrims must rely only on themselves.

At one point we all stopped to buy needles and cotton to thread into a white wall of cotton. We did it, took the snaps, but were past trying to get through the language maze to the meaning of the ritual.

And by then time was falling apart. Someone said we had been climbing for eight hours but it felt like... I no longer knew. Nor did June. My mouth was so dry it felt glued solid. But we just kept going until everyone stopped at a derelict tea shop and food was passed around - everyone sharing the ubiquitous rice and curry; and from a flask, a couple of mouthfuls of the most delicious tea in the universe... 10 minutes' rest.

The woman with the stick, suffering herself, massaged June's leg muscles before rubbing Tiger Balm, or something like it, into her own legs. Earlier, it seemed hours or maybe days ago, demure eyebrows had raised when the woman and June had joined in an impromptu dance with a party of 17-year-old lads who were making easy work of the descent. Our usual fierce independence was fracturing and softening round the edges as we felt the benign force of the community: everyone had to be looked after, everyone had to make it to the top - stopping was not an option and neither was leaving anyone behind.

"Listen," said Wasala in the remote hours of the night.

"It is not far now - you can hear the monks."

Just faintly, edging inside the jungle noises, was the chant. Sri Pada, the Sacred Footprint. It was near. The agony was over. All the other false finishes, the night mirages of mistaking a high-above resting places for the monastery, were forgotten. This was it.

And then we rounded a bend and looked up…and saw the pilgrim lights, high above, some curving away to the left and others to right going almost vertical, an impossible spiral into the night sky. The blow felt physical.

"We'll never make it," I breathed to June. "Never," she agreed as we just stared at it.

In the numbness of fatigue, the realisation grew that there was no other course but to go on. No going down. No stopping. No chance of making it to the top.

"Do we take the left route or the right?" I asked. No one answered. Perhaps no one understood my question. Maybe some of them were as shocked as us. But then I understood…there was just one trail: the lights curving out of sight on the left hopelessly high above us were on the lower part and they dropped with the mountain trail, vanishing from sight, until, finally, they lurched upwards in a punishing climb to the summit.

It was at that moment that everything changed. There was just the mountain, just life, and going on - the doubts just disappeared, not replaced by confidence or even hope, just not there; the inevitability of going on, never going back, simply existed in my stilled mind without emphasis or affirmation.

We started climbing again, weary step after weary step, rarely looking up to see how far but conscious of the monks' chant growing louder.

The group was sticking together: a helping hand here, several helping hands there…the cameras and water bag were back on my shoulder, biting into muscles, competing with the dull ache in my knees. And then, over the left curve of lights, down, down, down until the ground whipped up in a final ascent to the peak - what seemed like a million steps with a handrail, electrified in places where the lights touched it, to help arms haul flagging bodies to the top.

We were too tired to be amazed when we reached the top. It was about 6am, and we had taken twice the six or seven hours that fit young men can achieve: climbing for 13 hours, awake for 24 hours, and sunrise was scheduled for half an hour later. We took off our shoes and, with the others, walked on the icy floor round the top of the peak until we followed our group of pilgrims into the shrine of the Sacred Footprint. The people before us gave the customary small gifts of money, knelt before the footprint with hands together, and bowed three times to touch it with their supplicant hands and foreheads.

I bent, in the way of respectfully approaching a Buddha image and went to pass on but the attendant forcefully took my arm, showing me the right way…I knelt, hands together, and went forward three times to touch the footprint with my forehead and hands. June followed, carrying out the ritual without prompting, and we walked down the steps and on to the main concourse where Singalese and tourists from around the world vied for position to see the sunrise.

The sun eased over the horizon as the *poya* moon hung in the north-western sky, all our party now safely at the footprint, and we tried to tell them that we wanted to leave before them for the descent to catch the dawn light for our photographs. But, as we slipped away, the others were preparing to come too. If you believe in chance, then we chanced upon one of the truly captivating aspects of Sri Pada - the peak's dawn shadow, cast on the clouds between two lower mountains, looked like a ghost peak in greys and pinks.

Revived by the experience at the top and the beauty of the ghost mountain, we began the numbing descent with the same serious intent of the climb. Near the bottom, I looked back and up at Sri Pada. The cloud was gathering round the peak, round the Sacred Footprint, and the sun was lighting it up like a halo.

The tourist snapped it for the collection. But the accidental pilgrim marvelled at the sight and the night that made the confusion of life as clear as day.

Life with Maura
Brian Kellock (1999)

Our four-wheel-drive Isuzu bumps up the unmade road to Maura's single-storey house, one of several set back among the trees on either side. The cream-coloured clay of the track, now hard and crumbling but doubtless soft and slippery in the rainy season, contrasts with the lush greens of the trees. Mango, juayabano, baumbinga, coconut and star apple trees compete for space, displaying a rich variety of leaf patterns and colours. At first sight it is an idyllic scene, but it is one that forms the backdrop to a life of poverty and struggle of a kind that most rural Filipinos have to endure.

Maura and her husband Bonifacio, now in their 50s, do at least have land, which they inherited. To be more precise the land on which their ancestors squatted is now registered in their name for tax purposes; there is no title deed. If they were to leave for any time, someone else could move in and squat.

As we step from the truck, our idyllic view of the setting in which Maura, her husband and seven of her eight children live is disturbed only by the music from a hi-fi. The volume is soon turned down as the introductions begin. Other sounds take over; children shout as they play, a dog yaps and cockerels crow.

While Bonifacio works as a farmer on rented land, Maura runs her own little business buying the nuts of the cashew fruit which she shells, roasts and packs, and then sells on at a profit. On the tree the kidney-shaped nut is attached to the end of an edible yellow or orange fruit called the cashew apple. The seed at the centre of the nut is roasted before it can be eaten.

Maura and Bonifacio have lived on this plot of land since 1972. Until 1992 they lived and raised their family in a traditional house built of wood. Standing on low stilts like most older houses in the Philippines, it was roofed over with the long feathery leaves of the Nipa palm, the traditional roof covering gathered from swamps and river estuaries.

That house built of local wood has now gone. In its place is a new three bedroomed single-storey home built on solid foundations and made of breeze block topped with a corrugated metal roof. The materials were bought, little by little, out of savings and profits from the cashew nut business until Maura could afford to have someone build the house for them.

The three bedrooms off the long living room sleep nine; Maura and her husband, one married daughter and her husband who are waiting for a home of their own to be finished, and five other children, the youngest of them thirteen. On the back of the living room a recent addition is a small kitchen with a wood-burning stove used for cooking and for drying shelled nuts.

Although it is bright daylight outside, the living room is lit by a fluorescent tube fixed to a wooden support beam directly below the visible corrugated roof. Everything is clean and tidy, the walls are emulsioned a cream colour. On a stool in the centre of the room a large electric fan stands still. Pale green print curtains cover the doorways between the living room and the three bedrooms.

The same material is over the glassless wooden-frame or breeze-block latticed windows to the outside. A latticed breeze block serves as a window between the living room and the kitchen. A smart clock hangs on the wall. Outside, the walls of the house are rough and unrendered.

From here the wooden windows can be seen to be slatted, giving some protection during the rains. In a narrow strip of earth against one wall, Maura has planted a green garden of ferns and variegated leaves. More ferns grow in pots hanging from the wall.

Most of the rest of the 994 square metres of Maura's inheritance is hard earth planted here and there with shade-giving broad-leaved trees. Four piglets scurry to the exposed teats of their mother as she lies dead to the world under her own very large blue-and-white striped awning. The sow is tethered to a pole supporting the awning.

Nearby a strolling cockerel is also tethered. Maura's livestock of two sows, one boar, eight small piglets will sell for 500 *pesos* when weaned, four middle-sized piglets to feed the family at fiesta time, three hens, six roosters, three dogs, many cats and one cow.

I got an idea of what the old house was like from a wooden hut on low stilts still standing at the back of the house. Here Maura and some of her helpers work. The front half of the building is open on three sides, with some protection given by removable shuttering. The back half of the building is enclosed and dark; here the nuts are stored the year round.

Maura and several other younger relatives or neighbours are working together here. One sits on the ground in front of the hut cutting the raw nuts in half in their shells using a guillotine. Three others, sitting or squatting on the slatted work-floor, prise the seeds from their shells using metal gouges. The liberated nuts are placed into shallow oval cane-and-string baskets in which they are left in the open to dry before being baked. They are packaged and packed in 65 kilo sacks ready to be taken to the airport on a hired motorcycle or jeepney.

British Isles & Europe

Hay being dried, north Finland (photo: Michael Bell)

From Skye to Lewis
Insa Thierling (1996)

The first day of my first longer cycling tour the train is late, the ferry is late, and the road leading north from Arrandale runs uphill. The term "travelling light" has never been associated with me, so I have to struggle. There is no chance of reaching Sligachan before dark, but tiredness overcomes me anyway, so I stop at a B&B in the middle of nowhere, which seems much nicer than an overcrowded youth hostel or a campsite.

The next day is beautiful. I cycle around the rock of Mull, a route that offers marvellous views over the neighbouring islands. It is very hot for August, and I soon find myself sunburnt. The midges are pretty nasty here, too! The way to Portree is fantastic - it's downhill for miles and miles, and behind every corner the view gets more amazing. I have planned to spend a couple of days in Skye, hoping to make it to Dunvegan Castle. But I change my mind. There are moments when I feel deeply ashamed of my fellow Germans. Especially when, at 10pm, they choose to entertain the entire campsite with German-language rock music. Why can't I have them deported to Ibiza?

There are just too many people here at the moment, so the next day I pack up and head towards Uig. The game "spot the local" soon becomes boring, because it seems to be a hopeless pursuit. To my utter surprise, in a supermarket in the outskirts of Portree, I hear someone speaking Gaelic. There is hope! After all, one of my reasons for coming here was to get some language practice. Against all expectations, it takes me only one hour to get to Uig, and after cycling for miles through beautiful landscape, backpackers storm the place and order massive amounts of tea and coffee. By the time we reach Lochmaddy in North Uist, it's dark. And it's pouring. To top it all, I lose my way, and it takes me half an hour to find the youth hostel. The shower is alive with mould. Yuk.

The next morning brings more rain. But I am brave, and determined to make it to South Uist today. On the way I stop to see the chambered cairn of Barpa Langais, and Poball Fhinn (Finn's People), a very interesting stone circle that has fern growing all over its centre, but none at all growing on its outside. And there's a strange kind of feel to the place. I stop again at Clachan for some food, but as I leave the shop, the rain has worsened. I choose to wait under a sheltered bus stop, and a friendly local comes up and we have a chat. After 15 minutes or so I decide to go on after all. But I don't get too far, as after three hours of cycling through ceaseless rain, the water starts seeping through the seams of my jacket, and my so-called waterproof shoes give up the ghost - they are soaked through. Although it's only just 12.30pm, I stop at the next best B&B. I am dripping. The landlady is an absolute darling, lets me in and dries my stuff above the Aga.

Of course, the sun is shining again within minutes of my arrival. The landlady searches the house and then finds me a pair of trainers so I can go out and cycle over the causeway to the small island of Baleshare. As I spot the next wave of rain clouds in the sky, I make my way back.

There are loads of causeways the next day, as I cross Benbecula to South Uist. The landscape is beautiful. Somehow in these islands the grass is greener, the sky is bluer and the sheep are whiter. I soon reach South Uist (for Benbecula is flat!) whose Catholicism becomes immediately visible by quite a few statues of Mary. Unfortunately she doesn't hear my prayers for protection from the midges. By the time I reach the independent hostel in Howmore, I am well bitten. Tobha Mor is a former blackhouse with no hot water. There's a motley crowd of folks in the hostel including a brain surgeon and a guy from the Netherlands who teaches us Dutch swearwords, much to everyone's amusement. I also meet a very friendly German couple who have planned pretty much the same route as I. We'll see who makes it to Harris first.

Everyone takes the next day off to explore the beautiful beach, the mountains and the old cemetery behind the house. The peace is only occasionally disturbed by a local youth racing his motorbike over the dunes. In the evening, we gather again around the small Morso oven in the kitchen, our only source of heat, boiling pot after pot of water for tea to keep ourselves warm.

The next day is lovely, and the wind is in my back. Just before I reach Benbecula again, I stop to take a breath after some uphill cycling. But it is the landscape that takes a breath: it takes mine! I've never seen a pool as blue as the one I'm looking at now. It's the kind of view you want to keep in your memory rather than on a photo, so I leave the camera in the bag. I just can't stop looking and stand there for about a quarter of an hour. Before returning to the friendly B&B, I take a turn to go and see Teampull na Trionaid (Trinity Temple), the ruin of a medieval monastic settlement. A sheep tries to steal my sandwiches, but

I manage to scare it off. Later I find out that the landlady is a Gaelic speaker, but my hopes of having a nice conversation with her are destroyed by the arrival of two Swabians. But they are genuinely nice and I forgive them.

The next day takes me back to Lochmaddy harbour. The landlady has arranged to have my luggage taken there by car, and cycling along the newly-built road without it is almost like flying! I meet the Germans from Tobha Mor on the ferry, and within a few hours we find ourselves in Harris. There is a mountain path from Tarbert to Rhenigidale, the remotest of the island hostels, which they are going to take. As it looks like rain and I don't know what sort of terrain this path leads through, I decide not to take a risk and choose the 13-mile road. The worst of uphill struggles lies before me. It's raining, to top it all.

There is no B&B by the roadside, for this is the middle of nowhere. Fortunately, there are more frustrated cyclists around, so we push the bikes up together for a while. Then I say goodbye to them and take the turn to Rhenigidale. Another eight miles! The Street plunges very steeply down to almost sea level - a test for my brakes, and they cope brilliantly considering the road is not only steep but also wet. Down in the valley, there is a turn. And after this turn begins the strip of a constant 12% gradient. It goes on for miles and miles. At every corner I try to cheer myself up by telling myself, after that turn there'll be a bit of level road at least. But it just doesn't happen. Until all of a sudden, the road slopes down with a gradient of 13%. At the end of it, there's the hostel. At last! And hurrah! - there's a shower, and a friendly Australian who makes me a cup of tea. Two hours later, my German friends arrive, dripping with water and sweat. We don't last very long that evening.

In the morning, Fiona the Australian takes us on a tour of the island in her car. Harris is probably one of the most interesting Hebridean islands because of its contrasting landscapes. The west coast has an almost Mediterranean feel to it. Were it not for the mountains in the background with the dark clouds above them, on a sunny day like this one might easily believe oneself in the Algarve. We just can't get over the beauty of Luskentyre Beach and take lots of pictures. Fiona takes us on to Rodel church, the burial place of many illustrious MacLeod chiefs and a famous Gaelic poet. There are some very interesting slabs.

After lunch we make our way back to Tarbert by the east coast, which stands in an amazing contrast to the west. The landscape formed by oddly-shaped rocks looks an ideal setting for a *Star Trek* episode -

which would do the island a lot less damage than the proposed superquarry!

In Tarbert we say goodbye to Fiona who travels on to Uist. We take the mountain path back to the hostel in beautiful weather. Thank Heaven I took the bike along the road, or I would have got myself into some dangerous situations. After three hours of climbing, descending, climbing again, and striding through the heather, we reach our hostel again. Once again, we go for the "Special Rice" dinners that are found in every island backpacker's survival kit.

The next day is a Sunday, and we spend it in peace and quiet, walking, drawing, chatting and making lots of hot drinks because the Morso is too small to heat the room properly. We realise that the people who run the hostel must be Catholic: they dry their laundry outside! A few miles further north, the more fervent advocates of Hebridean Calvinism would very much disapprove of these "heathen practices".

On Monday morning we all set off for Lewis, and we arrange to meet again at the independent hostel in Garenin in two days' time. After looking at the map, I think I might not get as far as Stornoway, but somehow it works out in the end. Lewis is all purple with heather, which makes a lovely colour scheme with the green grass, the black peat, and the blue sky. Unfortunately, the blue doesn't last. By the time I reach the outskirts of Stornoway, my feet are wet again.

After a long search, I find a B&B, and funnily enough the landlady knows quite a few Lewis people I know. She, too, is incredibly friendly, and lets me leave my tent in the house until I come back from Garenin. On the way there, I stop in Shawbost to see the school museum and to have a look at a knitter's shop a friend has told me about. It is a really hot day, and I am eternally grateful as Sandra, the knitter, offers me a Coke and biscuits. Then I find that she has a blue jumper exactly the shade of that pool in South Uist. I don't care about further luggage, I must have that jumper! Sandra and I keep on chatting for over an hour and, of course, she, too, knows people I know. Slightly sunburnt, I reach Garenin in the early evening.

The hostel is well in German hands, the "Special Rice" is simmering away, clothes are drying on the pulley above the trusty Morso, and it all looks very atmospheric. But what is even more atmospheric is that night's sunset. (Of course, my camera made a black-ish mess of it.) One of the founders of the hostel has come to stay for the night. He's been coming here for many years, and he says he's never seen a sunset like it. Neither have we. The sea is turquoise and the sky is shaded in pink, orange and purple. There's a white ship on the horizon. It all looks like a kitschy postcard of the Caribbean, without the palm trees. We stand and watch in amazement until the sky turns black.

The next day, I head for the Carloway Broch, then for the Standing Stones of Callanish. It's relatively early, and I only meet two friendly hippies who, like me, are soaking up the atmosphere of this ancient sacred site. But within 15 minutes, "all the energy is ****ed until tomorrow morning", as one of the hippies puts it, by the arrival of a German coach party who spill over the field and are forced to listen to their rather spiritless tour guide. The hippies run off while I take the last few pictures, always trying to avoid bits of multicoloured waterproof jackets sticking out behind the stones.

The local archaeologist arrives with a group of Americans who keep on shouting how marvellous it all is, and disregarding the signs that ask visitors not to step on to the stones to avoid erosion; she puts them right on to the centre circle. I flee; on the way back I have to take shelter in the archaeologist's garage museum. On the walls, there are displays of the findings of her research (some of them slightly obscure, I find), and she also has a video of "Callanish through the Seasons" with a very soppy New Age harp soundtrack. Her American friends find it all marvellous.

I make my way back to the Carloway village shop. The shopkeeper is very friendly and tells me to try the Gaelic radio station in Stornoway for some Gaelic practice. He gives me the address and the names of some people to speak to. Bless him! The next day, we visit the loomshed of the man who runs the hostel. He shows us how the famous tweed is woven, and we all buy pieces of fabric and socks knitted by his wife.

The following day, I take the Pentland Road to Stornoway. It runs right across the island, and again it's all heather, lochs and peat, and the clearest air one can possibly imagine. I breathe in as deeply as I can, hoping to preserve some of it to take back to the mainland. At the Stornoway B&B, the door is half open. As no one answers when I knock, I just walk in. That very moment the landlady comes out of the kitchen and says: "I've just been thinking of you, and here you are now!" Second sight exists.

I leave my stuff and make my way to Radio nan Gaidheal. I am given a tour of the studios, and then I am let loose to speak Gaelic to people. Funnily enough one of the researchers recognises me: "You were in Barra with the Celtic Society at Easter!" I'm invited again for the next morning's live programme. Fortunately, there is no time for me to be interviewed! But they talk to one of my lecturers over the phone, and when he's off air, I am handed earphones and a mike to speak to him. It feels rather surreal. Everyone is really nice, and Aonghas keeps making me one cup of tea after the other. Christine gives me the number of one of my favourite Gaelic poets (who invited me for lunch a month later and helped me a lot with my dissertation). Success!

In the evening there's the farewell parade of the local Highland Regiment, which is to be disbanded. The place is crowded with people watching the kilted men playing their pipes and drums. The next morning I have to leave. I have just enough money left to get me back to Glasgow where, with two hours' delay, I arrive at midnight. I fall asleep very fast, dreaming of heather and sunsets and sheep.

Fasnacht in Basle
Hedva Anbar (2001)

If you plan to be in the vicinity of Basle, in the north-west corner of Switzerland adjacent to France and Germany, try to get there at the beginning of March, so that you can experience Fasnacht. This annual three-day festival, a Protestant adaptation of the Roman Catholic carnival, takes place a week later during Lent in an atmosphere which fuses ritual with abandon, discipline with chaos and sophisticated artistry with childish mischief. Fasnacht grants the city's inhabitants - modest, restrained, courteous and laid back throughout most of the year - a licence for exhibitionism, inquisitiveness, jealousy, malice and other equally alien behaviour traits.

Buy a gold, silver or bronze *Blagedde* (badge), representing the Motto (theme which usually has a specifically local significance) chosen for that year and wear it as a sign of support. Get up early on Monday morning and make your way to the Marktplatz in front of the 16th-century Town Hall where the festivities start at the stroke of 4.00am. The street lights are extinguished and the *Morgenstraich* (morning parade) starts. *Cliques* (groups) appear from all directions, flautists and drummers in magnificent costumes, their feet in clogs, outrageous masks on their faces and lighted lanterns, decorated to represent the themes selected by the different *cliques*, on their heads.

The members of the cliques change their outfits and masks before they assemble for the cortege at 1.30pm on Monday afternoon. This time they follow pre-planned routes through the city streets, together with *Guggenmusig* (brass band) musicians playing out-of-tune but recognisable pieces on old dented instruments, and floats with Waggis from neighbouring Alsace who throw fruit, vegetables, sweets and confetti at the spectators. *Clique* representatives distribute *Schnitzelbangg* (satirical verse) in the local Swiss-German dialect, which has no agreed system of spelling, on the *clique* themes. On Monday evening all the lanterns are displayed in the Münsterplatz in front of the Minster, where they remain for the following two days, groups rove through the streets entertaining the crowds and crowds invade the local restaurants to order traditional flour soup and listen to *Schnitzelbangg*.

On Tuesday the *clique* members put on the costumes they wore the previous year and the children's parade takes place. In the evening there are concerts in the city's main squares, where each brass band is allocated a ten minute slot. On Wednesday there is another cortege and again groups rove through the streets and crowds fill the restaurants until Fasnacht ends at 4.00am or 5.00am on Thursday.

Enjoy yourselves but don't forget yourselves. Bear in mind the injunctions in the leaflet distributed by the Basle Tourist Office: "by all means laugh and have fun, but remember, half masks, painted faces, false noses and *Narrenkappen* (fools' headgear) are frowned upon...don't pick any confetti up from the street...refrain from talking during a recitation even if you fail to understand it or find it funny."

As spectators you will have three days of fun. For the insiders, Fasnacht is a year-round activity. After a short break they will again start meeting regularly to choose the following year's theme and get it agreed by the Fasnacht committee, design new costumes, design new masks and lanterns, write new verses, practise the flute and drum, prepare for concerts and enjoy the comradeship of kindred spirits from the inner core of Basle society.

Trip to the North
Michael Bell (2002)

This summer I went to Scandinavia, one of the richest parts of the world, and saw things which are as interesting as you could find anywhere. I found it more interesting because it relates better to what I know at home than what I see in more alien countries.

I drove all the way by car, 6,000 miles, so the roads were a large part of the experience. Danish roads are a delight; modestly but well built, they allow slightly tighter turns and steeper gradients than other national standards (but there's no problem about that) and so even two-lane roads can have flyovers, beautifully fitted into the rolling Danish countryside without the monumentalism and extravagant use of land which so disfigures roads everywhere else in Europe. Making the secondary roads so good means that traffic is not drained onto the main roads. It is true that the small size of the population means that traffic is not very heavy (the big new bridge between Sjæland and Fyn is only two lanes each way), but a large part of the pleasant experience is due to good design, which creates civilised behaviour. The best roads on the trip! But even Danish signposting didn't come up to British standards.

Roads in Norway are endlessly turning and sloping. The natural speed is 50mph, so people drive well spaced out and make no attempt to overtake. Very relaxing! In the far north, the road is broken by ferries. The ferries are interesting vessels in their own right. For the shorter journeys, up to about 30 minutes, they are double-ended, with propellers and rudders at both ends. It was a lot of fun to work out how they were steered. Some journeys are up to 1½ hours, and are an opportunity for travellers to talk to each other as the ship passes through this amazing scenery. One of the unexpected delights of the Norwegian road is the flowers that bloom along the roadside, mostly lupins; I had no idea they grew so far north.

There are fewer ferries than there were on the last occasion I was in Norway, 30 years ago. A cheap method of tunnelling through rock has obviously been invented and tunnels have been built to avoid ferries, not mostly by tunnelling under the sea, but using tunnels to re-arrange the routes so that they avoid high ground which gets covered with snow in winter, and avoiding slopes which are liable to avalanche in the spring. Tunnelling technique has obviously advanced; all tunnels have very roughly finished walls, but some have water pouring in from the roof, poor lighting and a road surface with lots of loose stone on it. A hairy experience, and some tunnels are forbidden to cyclists. The longest I went through was 600 feet under sea level joining the mainland to the island of Magerøya - North Cape is on its northern tip. That was a good tunnel. There are underground roads with underground roundabouts on them under Tromsø!

We might moan about "overcrowding" at home, but plenty of space also has its price. In the far north, signposts not only name the places, they show the way to the nearest hospital. You can't expect an ambulance in 10 minutes in these places.

Midges are claimed to be a problem in Scandinavia, but they weren't; everybody said they had had a dry spring and midges were much fewer than usual. I noticed swallows as far North as Oulu, a kind of biological control? There was a little rain, "English weather," they said with a smile, such a pretty compliment to my home country, but if they had seen real English rain they wouldn't have said that. It was amazingly hot; I was in shorts to well north of the Arctic Circle. Only in the last few hundred miles did it get chilly. North Cape itself has a tourist trap "visitor centre" at the very tip, but the magic of the place was unaffected. A rocky headland, with dark waters below. (All water seems dark in the north, probably because the light strikes it at a grazing angle.) It is only 1,200 miles from the North Pole, far less than the distance I had already come, and I was struck by the thought that the midnight sun here was the midday sun in Alaska, shining over the top of the world.

Although the midnight sun can only be fully seen north of the Arctic Circle, no-darkness extends far south of that. No-darkness was a more interesting experience than I had expected. There was no deadline on anything! I could do anything at any time I chose. Wake, sleep, eat, move along! And the same applies to the people who live here. Children can come in from school, go straight to bed, be up and out to play in the street at 3 in the morning, come in, do their homework and be at school at 8. The adults are likewise free to plan their day as they please, go to work, dig the garden (and I saw gardens only 10 miles south of North Cape!), paint the house, at the times it suits them. I asked about what it was like in winter: many said that for a few hours around "midday" there was a very beautiful light from the south, a kind of post-sunset glow, though for the rest of day and when it was overcast it was completely dark. I was interested in how they coped in this winter darkness, but they seemed untroubled by that; they didn't seem to grasp my interest in the question. "We have electric light and we carry on as normal," they said. And indeed I began to understand this. When I got south into Germany, I was caught short by nightfall. I had come to expect continuous light, I had failed to plan for that predictable event, sunset! That's a lesson I will take home with me - to plan for night and be less bound by the clock.

All the Northern countries make a lot of Midsummer Day; it is a family celebration, like Christmas is for us. I went to the municipal party in Rovaniemi. The Finnish flag was raised and the national anthem "Our land" was sung, a more modest and less bombastic melody than any other I have heard. Then on came the mayor, a parody of a shabbily dressed politician in an old raincoat, though there wasn't a cloud in the sky, and he gave a speech. Finnish has an unfortunate tendency to sound like the "Duckspeak" of George Orwell's *1984* anyway, but the mayor carried it to an extreme. It took careful listening to realise that his quacks consisted of single words, with their remorseless initial stress, each of which stands for several words in English, separated by long periods of silence. But the audience listened, even laughed. Then he changed into English, and read out the poem which had raised the laughter - I hadn't realised it was a poem. "What is a Finn? He is a man who doesn't answer when questioned. And who answers when not questioned." (I have to say this is completely contrary to my experience of Finns; they chat in a wholly normal way.) He read it in the normal flowing English way. We mock and imitate other languages: it's things like this that give you a hint of what English must sound to those whose mother tongue it is not.

Then on came a singing and dancing group. First was carried on a portable harmonium. This is a box about 4 ft long x 18" wide x 18" deep, with handles at both ends, so that it can be carried between two people. The top folds up to reveal a keyboard and the bottom folds down to form legs and pedals for the player to pump the wind. There was some bother finding a level place on the rocks to stand it. It was played by a woman every bit of whose appearance and manner screamed "schoolteacher!" Short neat hair, neat suit (in a country where formal dressing is rare), nimble little white shoes, authoritative manner in directing the singers. They led the crowd in obviously well-known songs, then they did some folk-dance turns, and then some really quite raunchy song, dance and mime routines. And then the "schoolteacher" surprised me. She stood up, and to the beat of a reverberating Lappish magic drum she sung a *yoik*, with its catches in the voice, sudden changes of voice quality and notes between the notes of the keyboard. .

Very spooky! A *yoik* is a personal song saying who you are and what you are like. And who was she? Never judge a book by its cover!

Folk music is one of my enthusiasms, so I went to the Haapavesi folk festival. It wasn't only the music that opened my eyes. Walking along to the festival, it sudddenly struck me that they all had "naked faces". This struck a chord in me, because I had recently gone through a sort of personal crisis in a music gathering back home when I saw that a particular woman had a "naked" face. When she wasn't thinking anything, her face relaxed into an expressionless look which might seem sad. But when she did think something, surprise, doubt, sympathy, anger, it showed clearly. Even across the other side of the room, when I couldn't hear a word of the conversation, its general tenor could be noted by watching her face. It takes courage to let others see what you are thinking. By contrast, her husband's default expression was "cheery chappie" and, for the first time in years, I saw that not as an expression of normal cheerfulness, but as a mask to hide his inner self from people who might take advantage of him if they knew what he was thinking.

Years ago, I had made up my mind that I would not be a coward, I would be honest with people. But, over the years, my courage had trickled away and I had come to put on a mask like everybody else, like this woman's husband. So it was a revelation to see that in Finland, she would be in the majority, and he would seem to be wearing a mask of inscrutability, as Chinese seem to us. Most of us put on clothes, walk and body language, facial expression, to shield ourselves from the insight of others. In Finland, that is simply lacking. What does that say about us? And about the Finns?

For some reason, the Finns have taken to Argentinian tango music; it has dominated Finnish popular music for years. Argentinians and Italians can earn a good living playing "real" tango music in Finland. The Finns' interest seems straightforward enough, they like the excitement and glamour of the music. But I wonder how it seems to Argentinians? In their troubles, does it seem any kind of comfort that this small country at the other end of the world takes such an interest in them? And what do they think of the Finns, with their complete lack of pose? Excellent or simply children?

And before I got to the music there were other strangenesses. There was a stage in the main hall, with seats in front of it. In any other country, the gangway would be set at right angles to the stage, but here it was at 60° to the stage - and it looked right! Finland is like that, there are touches of exquisite care and taste; in what other country would you see sheet metal triangles mounted on pylons to make the best of these engineering structures? But it had gaps. Some of their building and roads design and upkeep would seem shameful by British standards. It wasn't helped by the fact that in our green and pleasant land, bare earth gets covered by grass in a few weeks, but in Finland with its cold and lack of rain, bare earth stays bare. It looks untidy!

All over the North, history and culture generally get a lot of attention. There are some impressive medieval castles, now furnished as museums, with very interesting exhibits, laid out in a scholarly way and usually described in English as well. The castles were rebuilt a lot, leading to interesting changes of space, and they survived into the age of guns, so they are very thick-walled and this opened my eyes to the use of space. In their later use as official residences, the windows were opened up and bench seats set into the thickness of the walls, so that you could sit in a rather enclosed space within the wall with the window, with its stunning view on one side and a large room on the other side, and it felt unusual and pleasant. In Iran, there is a tradition of verandahs overlooking gardens. It feels very pleasant, but the effect is much reduced by having a balustrade, so there is none. (To make it hard for small children to climb up to the verandah and fall off, the steps up are made very high. But even so, it's a mother's nightmare.) Is there an architectural theory of space to explain this, in the way that music theory explains how mood is changed by changes in harmony?

We think Stonehenge is ancient; it is 5,000 years old. Whatever rites were performed there, no Christian site can have had the time to equal its record. It is even older than the pyramids. But even Stonehenge cannot match Alta. Alta was occupied as soon as the ice melted, 12,000 years ago. The rocks are carved with drawings, rather shallow scratchings on the rock, nowadays highlighted with ochre as they probably were in the past. It is an open-air museum; you wander around on paths in the sunshine and look at these match-stick drawings of men and women and animals and fish. They speak to us far more than the blank stones of Stonehenge. Some of the symbols have lived on in Lappish culture and appear on their magic drums. I know of no other such ethnic or cultural continuity in Europe or the world. The Lapps (called "Sami" in their own language and the Nordic languages) are a branch of the same stock as the Finns, who are very aware of it and their connections with the other people of the north of Russia and Finnic peoples who have been surrounded by Russians as they spread northwards from what is now Serbia. You see many books about the plight of these peoples. The Finns don't seem very interested in the

Hungarians, who seem to return the lack of interest. We don't take such an interest in North Germany where we English came from.

The bookshops were a revelation. Such a range! The ice-age prehistorical novels of Jean M Auel (in translation) were always prominent. Not too surprising in countries where everybody is so aware that theirs were covered with ice not very long ago. The best bookshop I saw was Stockmann's in Helsinki. It had a bigger range of English books than you would see in even a large London bookshop and a rather different range. And that's just the English books, there were Swedish books and German books and French books and of course Finnish books. And obviously a public to buy them. It makes our world of English-only thought and language look very much a backwater.

I took the ferry to Sveaborg/Suomenlinna (many Finnish places are named in both languages; I loved the sound of these words), the chain of island fortresses outside Helsinki harbour. I was drinking in the bar with only the barman for company, and in came a group of men. The barman told me that one of them, his boss, had bought me a drink. So I went and joined them, there were some foreigners among them and luckily they all spoke good English. A Mexican among them, 12 years resident in Finland, agreed with everything I said about their faces - he thought Finns were charming. We had a meal, we went on a pub-crawl, they told me they were a group of gays (I would probably have guessed in the end even if they hadn't told me) and we had the most interesting conversations. In fact, one of the truly good things about the North is that you can have an intelligent conversation with most people if you have a common language. One of them worked in Stockmann's bookshop and he had a wonderful perk - he could take the books home to read so long as he returned them in saleable condition. Even he felt overwhelmed by the number of good and worthwhile books. Life is too short!

The most obviously gay man, with a completely shaven head and a very mobile face, was the only person I met who "lied with his face". He said he had served in the French Foreign Legion, he said he worked for the police, etc...each of these unlikely, impossible to believe in combination; and when he finished saying these things he gave a "believe me" smile, but I soon disbelieved everything he said. Straightness is not just a sexual orientation, it's a taste for the truth though, to be fair, some of the others showed signs of irritation at this man's fabulations.

My fellow tourists were an interesting bunch too. There was the amazingly self-sufficient German student cyclist who baked his own

*Midnight music (above); Helsinki gay group, with "Foreign Legionnaire"
in foreground (photos: Michael Bell)*

bread. There was the French couple who remembered the battle of Narvik from their childhood; they were going to visit this battlefield. They had kept copies of *Paris Match* from that time. The Allies were winning this battle and only left the field to help France, but France fell anyway two weeks later. There were the Russians (not a popular nationality in Finland!) who had bought second-hand cars in Germany and were driving them home through Finland to avoid travelling through Poland because they were liable to be attacked in Poland. To avoid that, some Russians (presumably professional car-dealers) drove their second-hand cars through Poland in convoy. And Poland is going to join the EU soon!

I am pleased to be able to say that, as an Englishman, I was made very welcome wherever I went. That is, when they had confirmed that I was English; to speak the language does not show that you are of that nationality.

Finally, why "the North"? "Scandinavia" may be originally a Scandinavian name, taken up by the Romans, but it now appears as a foreign word in Scandinavia. The current native name for the region is "Norden". This means literally "The North", and was so translated into English until about 1910. ("Nord" means "north" and the "-en" ending means "the". This is part of the general system in which "en mann" means "a man", but "mannen" means "the man". There are different endings for the different genders and plurals.) The word "Nordic" is a Frenchification of the derived adjective "Nordisk", literally "Northish". Whether Finland, with its very different language, but rather similar general culture, counts as "Scandinavia" or "Nordic" is a matter for endless debate, but politically and culturally, that is the way it has chosen to align itself.

Where Am I? In the Village
Neil Matthews (1995)

The file is slammed down on the desk and he strides out of the office, back to freedom. The accelerator feels good beneath his feet as the car eats up the miles. He is unaware that another car is following...as he packs a suitcase in his flat, a feeling of wooziness overwhelms him. His last conscious thought is: gas. He awakes on the floor, pulls back the curtains and sees...

I have a theory that part of the reason for the popularity of *The Prisoner* lies in its expression of a wish which we've all harboured from time to time: to walk away from a job, telling our employers to get stuffed. Or, then again, maybe not. But, having seen the TV series, a chance to visit the location for its filming, Portmeirion in North Wales, was too good to miss.

If only somebody had done the same for my wife Helen and me as they did for Patrick McGoohan and spirited us straight to Portmeirion. As it was, we struggled up the M40 through hail and driving gales, pausing only to shudder as the lorry in front of us overturned...still, the rest of the journey was pleasant, passing through Shropshire on our way over the border. The Welsh road to the coast is long and winding and extremely pretty.

By this time, we were tired and ready for bed. The next morning, I pulled back the curtains in the living room and saw...well, not quite the same view as in *that* credit sequence. But it still sent a shiver down the spine.

The bell tower, just as steep and forbidding as expected; the dome (no longer green, due to a redecoration a few years ago); the Roman remains; the pool in the centre of the Village; all combined to produce a theatrical effect. It was hard not to think of the surroundings as a giant set, awaiting a cue, even in broad daylight. The architect of Portmeirion, Sir Clough Williams-Ellis, once said that he wanted "to show people, with a sort of light-opera approach, that architecture could be fun, could be entertaining, interesting, intriguing".

The Village is all of those things. If the art lies in concealing art, then the Village is a work of art; an architect weaving all the tricks of his trade, concealed by natural beauty. Look at the buildings, breathe in the

71

sea air, walk down to the estuary through the palm trees and you could be by an Italian lake. Yet one of the most startling qualities of Portmeirion is its ability to deceive. False perspectives, fake windows, life-size figurines are everywhere. Two-storey houses turn out to have only one floor. The walk up the hill is steeper than a casual glance might imply. Even the small shops have a vaguely unreal air to them; the assistants might be speaking fluent Welsh or, then again, perhaps they are not.

Although one can take a walk through the nearby woods or go down past the hotel to the stone boat near the estuary, everything revolves around the Village. Given enough sunlight, a peek through the Camera Obscura at the southern end of the resort will produce a clear image of the Village, as if viewed through a television camera...

It was a pity when the moment came to wave goodbye to Portmeirion - farewell to fantasy, back to drab reality. At least once in a lifetime, you should resign your top-secret job and come to see the Village. Who knows - you might never escape...

Look out for Nelson in Portmeirion
(photo: Helen Matthews)

Pixies, Ponies, Trolls and Goblins
Rae Kruft Welton (1998)

We had booked a cottage for two weeks in a village called Blönduós. As we soon found out, no-one had ever stayed that long in Blönduós before, and we quickly became local celebrities recognised wherever we went.

The wooden cottage we stayed in was small, but warm and comfortable. The warmth was particularly useful when the day after we arrived the temperature dropped to minus 10°C with a minus 10 wind-chill and it started to snow. I felt particularly betrayed by the sales brochure which had promised the June temperatures in Iceland to be around 13-15°. I bought a thick woolly green scarf, and we drove off around the coast to look at the scenery. Northern Iceland is spectacular. There are virtually no trees so the bones of the country are exposed. The way the clouds move and light changes across the land catches your attention, and there is an incredible sense of space. There are snow-capped peaks at every turn rising starkly out of the lava bedrock. I fell in love with it.

There is only one main road. It circles Iceland and is tarmacked most of the way round. The rest of it is packed dirt. Shaggy sheep and wanton ponies wander at random across the road, daring you to hit them (compensation is payable by the driver to the farmer). There are no edges and frequently there may be a drop of several hundred feet on one side, with nothing to tell you where the edge is in the fog except for widely spaced reflectors on small poles. There are other numbered roads too, and if the sign says "4-wheel drive only" then it really means it. The better ones are deep gravel and stone, with potholes you could lose your car in, and often have streams or small rivers running across them.

The weather improved after the first few days and it stayed at 11-15°C for the rest of our stay. The locals came out in daring T-shirts (we carried on wearing our coats) and some of them asked us if we'd been about for the unusual snowstorm the weekend before. I forgave the travel brochure for its weather misinformation, and Nick and I went horse riding.

Nick had not been on a horse since an unfortunate incident in Finland the year before, so he was particularly nervous. It didn't help when the horses were introduced as Dimmi (translating as Dusky) and Krappy (which apparently means Slushy Snow). Nick's feet nearly met under the pony's belly (he is 6"4') and his riding hat had to be tied on with string as his head was too large. Nick's plaintive cry to let him get off was ignored by our cheerful guide who didn't speak English. This may have been a good thing in the long run as once again the scenery was spectacular.

We rode down along the river Blönduós between two towering mountain ranges. Icelandic ponies are sure-footed and hardy, and wonderfully patient. Nick trailed behind, wary of encouraging Krappy to move faster than a walk. Krappy didn't seem to care, happy to go at his rider's pace. Nick slowly regained his confidence, and we both enjoyed ourselves.

In general the tourist industry hasn't really got the idea yet in Iceland. It takes a fair amount of courage to drive up to what looks like an abandoned warehouse, under the eyes of all the local children, knock on the door, and ask if there just happens to be an ancient shark-fishing vessel in there. As it happened, there was a whole museum of artefacts, from the first car in Iceland to shoes made out of fish-skin. Iceland does that to you a lot. You thought it was just an isolated petrol station on an empty road, but underneath it there is a whole shopping centre where you can buy sweets, woolly jumpers, travel maps, works by a local painter and some postcards to send home. It is incredibly expensive, though. Nearly everything is imported. A pint of beer or glass of wine cost about £5. Rumour has it that Icelanders take weekend shopping sprees to Glasgow, which cover the cost of their flight. I can believe it.

Up in a town called Húsavik, there are whale-watching tours out into the Arctic Sea. They claim to have a 96% success rate, which naturally I didn't believe until we got out into the far reaches of the bay. There is something magical about seeing the giants of the ocean. I have seen, with my own eyes. We saw about six minke whales before we were honoured by a display of the collective talents of a school of dolphins. They threw themselves out of the water racing in front of the boat, showing off, twisting and turning. I honestly think they were having more fun than the watchers. The boat staff provided warm mittens and hot coffee towards the end of the trip, just when we needed them.

Further round the coast from Húsavik and a few miles inland is a valley in the shape of a horseshoe. It goes by the name of Asbyrgi and it is said to be a hoof print of Sleipnir, the eight-legged steed of the

Norse God Odin. It has hundred-foot cliffs, a haven for nesting seabirds. Their calls echo around the valley. It is also one of the rare sheltered places in Iceland and consequently it is full of dwarf silver birch trees, undergrowth and mosses. That and the constant calls of the birds create a magical atmosphere where trolls and goblins might find shelter.

Reluctantly, we drove further inland along a cinder road only just reopened after the winter. They must get through a lot of hire-cars in Iceland, or there's a hot trade in new suspension systems. Eventually we got to Dettifoss, the most powerful waterfall in Europe. It thunders down between the sheer sides of a gully. You can feel the vibrations in your chest. In some respects it puts Niagara to shame - maybe because the Icelandic token towards tourism was a couple of organic looking toilets, and a flattish bit of rock to park on. There were no souvenir shops or restaurants, not even a kiosk to buy postcards from. It was genuinely unspoilt.

We struggled on down the road, occasionally getting up into third gear. I was glad to reach the main road again. The next stop was a volcano just outside the famous area of Mývatn. Mývatn means "midge lake". It is a green and beautiful area, with mounds of moss, and spiky boulders of lava sticking up out of the lake. The volcano caught my imagination though. It is supposed to be dormant, but the steam rising from the vents (fumeroles) makes you wonder. From the top you can see just where the black lava flowed last time it erupted, complete with flow marks like setting chocolate or icing-sugar on a cake. On the side of the mountain there are pools of boiling sulphurous mud, with cute little signs telling you not to stick your foot in there.

All the heating and hot water is powered by geothermal energy. In practice this means the water smells faintly of sulphur, which adds an interesting counterpoint to tea and coffee, and turns all your silver jewellery black. The tarnish does wear off eventually, but the Gods only know how Thor kept his hammer shiny!

We experienced another reason why geothermal energy is so convenient when we went white-water rafting down one of the glacial rivers so common in this part of the world. The rafting was fairly exciting without being too challenging. The water, as with all glacial rivers, was a luminescent turquoise colour. Half way down, just as we were starting to get cold, we pulled the rafts over to the bank and the guides produced a box out of a small cave in the ground. It had all the equipment for making cocoa in it, and the hot spring nearby produced near-boiling water, to provide the last ingredient. Set up for the rest of the journey, we accepted the challenge of leaping off a cliff-face into the river. It looks a lot further down from up there. I was sorry when the trip was over.

Back in Blönduós we walked on the black basalt beach and saw the midnight sun hanging in the sky with the full moon on the summer solstice. It never did get dark the whole time we were there. It was time to go. We waved goodbye, filled up with petrol, and pulled out of the petrol station up to the roundabout. With a sudden shock I realised I was on the wrong side of the road. A puzzled looking local drove past, recognised us and waved. I pulled out on to the roundabout, and Nick pointed out that I was also going round the roundabout the wrong way. I wobbled merrily on to the right side of the road. With this final piece of excruciating driving, we left Blönduós and headed for Reykjavik.

Reykjavik looks like pixie town from a distance. All the roofs of the houses are a different colour - red, green, blue - dotted about on the slopes. There are a couple of shopping streets, which makes it a veritable metropolis in Icelandic terms. The prices as everywhere were extortionate. Having said that, I liked Reykjavik. It was relaxed, the people were friendly and went out of their way to help us.

Some turf-roofed houses (photo: Rae Kruft Welton)

This Other Eden
Roger Boden (2002)

Before I had even reached Penzance to set sail on the ferry, I was prepared for the extravagant abundance of wildlife, as I realised I was travelling on the M5 during the height of the breeding season for traffic cones. These charming little creatures have multiplied greatly owing to a series of wet summers. There appear to be three main sub-species: the greater, the lesser and increasingly, the crested with a small yellow light on the top. They stand there for mile after mile in serried ranks, oblivious to the traffic, often blocking entire lanes for no apparent reason. Oddly, nobody seems to know their precise breeding location which is a closely guarded secret because, incredible though it may seem, some people wish them harm...but not everybody, and there are reported cases of some people keeping them as pets in their bedroom - although I deplore this practice as cones are sociable creatures.

Having left my car in Penzance, I boarded the *Scillonian III* for the 2½ hour voyage to Hugh Town, the capital, although it is little more than a village. It is situated on a narrow isthmus between the garrison and the rest of St. Mary's proper. All told, there are 140 islands and islets and St. Mary's is the largest, even so it is only two and a half miles long. Transport around St. Mary's is bus, taxi, bicycle or foot. It is almost impossible to get lost because, if you keep walking, you will end up back where you started.

To visit the Isles of Scilly is to travel back in time to the more leisurely pace of things I remember from my childhood in the 1950s. Strangers wish you "good morning" or "good afternoon". The hedgerows abound with familiar and exotic flowers and song birds that used to be abundant on the mainland are commonplace. Often, they are so tame that they will take food from your hand.

There is a delightful air of improvisation about life for the residents and, from the fumes coming the vehicles, I'll swear they run on paraffin. However, there are so few vehicles that air pollution is simply not a problem. There is nearly always a breeze or gale, but it hardly ever gets cold. Some snow fell in the 1980s and some of the older residents wouldn't venture out until the snow had gone.

Naturally, seafood is a popular item on the menu and, after several days of eating fish, I decided to ring the changes and headed for the Chicken Shack. I ordered a chicken curry, only to be told "Chicken's off." "But," I protested weakly, "This is the Chicken Shack...you can't be serious." At this point, I distinctly heard the word "sarcastic" above the murmur from the other diners and as I turned wild eyed, they all studiously looked at their plates and began eating rapidly. In the end, I had to settle for a Cornish pasty.

Another sight on St. Mary's which was once normal on the mainland is elm trees. Before this, the last time I saw a mature elm was in the early 1970s. Most days it was my custom to wander down to the quayside and decide which island to visit. I visited St. Agnes twice, including over the sand bar to the neighbouring island of Gugh, which is a nesting site for thousands of vociferous gulls. When I approached, I was reminded uncomfortably of Alfred Hitchcock's film *The Birds,* or maybe they had heard of my exploits at the Chicken Shack. St. Agnes has the reputation of being Britain's most south-westerly community and is achingly beautiful.

My visit to Tresco, the second-largest island, naturally included a visit to the famous sub-tropical abbey gardens. The variety of trees and plants from around the world is breathtaking. Bryher is the smallest inhabited island and lies alongside Tresco, divided from it by a narrow channel. It too has a dramatic beauty all of its own. St. Martin's became my favourite of the islands I visited with its hedged flower-growing fields stretching down to the sea. I will return one day, but I will be surprised if the Isles have changed very much.

A Taste of Georgia
Neil Harris (2000)

The sight of the helicopter as it sped in our direction, along the valley that leads from Omalo to Shtrolta, made me think of a scene from *M*A*S*H*.

Our rescue was at hand. Our trekking plans had already had to be altered as the Russian Airforce had "accidentally" bombed part of our intended route the previous week, missing Dagestan by quite a few miles. The risk of treading on unexploded ordnance was considered too high. I had decided on a trekking trip to Georgia as it promised adventure in an area little touched by tourism and scenery on the grand scale. I was not to be disappointed.

The Tusheti region of the Caucasus mountains borders Dagestan and Chechnya, both of which are currently thorns in the side of Moscow. To reach this little-visited area we had to fly to Tbilisi, the decaying but stylish capital of Georgia, then travel by coach across the fertile Georgian plain towards the Caucasus mountains. The sight of Soviet-era factories in various states of disrepair illustrated the parlous state of the Georgian economy. However, the abundance of produce grown in the region meant the locals looked healthy, if not wealthy.

Our first night was spent in the village of Alvani staying in the house of Maria, one of the Georgian guides supplied by Caucasus Travel, the local organisers. The evening meal, taken alfresco, introduced us to Georgian hospitality. This involved copious amounts of home-brew wine, mostly very palatable, and toasts to all and sundry.

After the meal a constitutional was called for, and as we could still walk in a straight line, we took a tour of Alvani. The main village crossroads proved depressing. It contained a Soviet-style culture centre that had been left to rot after independence, and also a couple of middle-aged vigilantes toting Kalashnikovs. Overnight we were treated to a dramatic display of thunder and lightning, little realising that this was not to be the last firework display we would witness.

Next morning dawned sunny and warm. Our transport for the journey up and over the 10,000-foot Bani Pass was to be an ex-Soviet Army six-wheel-drive lorry. Two planks, cushioned by foam, were to be our seats. The canyon-like valley that led up to the pass contained the remnants of the power supply that once fed Tusheti; alas now in a poor state, and unlikely to be restored in the near future. The road is built of compacted shale, and allows alarming views down sheer drops, but as there are no signs of crunched vehicles in the river bottom it must be safe. Honestly!

The sudden change from plain to mountains afforded great views south towards Tbilisi as we climbed out of the river valley into grassy highlands on the run in to the Bani Pass. The high point of the pass itself was tatty, a disappointment, with no indication that this was the only entrance to Tusheti by vehicle. A picnic lunch soon followed, and again the extent of Georgian hospitality became apparent, as a fortified wine, tasting like a cross between brandy and port, was passed around in a cup made from a horn. This brew was extremely moreish and allegedly made from the grapes once the season's wine had been trod.

The slow descent to Shtrolta was down another raw river valley, its sheer sides peopled by conifers, their roots grabbing the meagre soil for all their worth. The village of Shtrolta proved to be little more than half a dozen houses, but typical of many in the Tusheti region. Most of the people living there only visited the high pastures in the mountains during the summer, mainly to graze their animals and grow potatoes, returning to Alvani in October and leaving the fearsome weather of the mountains to the few wolves and bears that still populate Tusheti. Another night of Georgian hospitality followed, ending around a bonfire, the wine still flowing as midnight approached.

After another night in which the heavens opened and nature's fireworks were displayed, we were due to take our first trek. After a lung bursting climb (at this altitude there is only 75% of normal oxygen) lasting for about 4 hours, we arrived at a small lake well above the tree line. The alpine-like views across the Caucasus mountains more than compensated for the effort involved in the ascent. While some swam, I loafed, a large explosion from the direction of Dagestan piercing the tranquillity. So the Russian Airforce occasionally hits the right country! The descent back to Shtrolta was a knee-jerking experience for me, an old running injury returning to haunt me.

Georgian hospitality again showed itself, once we had bathed in the bathhouse fed from a nearby spring; the water ingeniously heated by a wood burning stove. The produce of the vine flowed as the toasts from our Georgian hosts got more emotional. Later on, lightning hinted at the deluge that would follow overnight.

Thursday dawned misty from the overnight rain, so our trip over a shallow pass to our campsite afforded only limited views. After fording a river, churning and high from recent rain, in our trusty Russian truck, we arrived in Dartlo, only to discover that the road to our intended campsite was blocked by a shale avalanche. Dartlo contained many of the famed Tusheti towers, now empty, which formed the main defence system of the region.

Our crew set up camp near to Dartlo, meanwhile we went for a short trek to Zemo Dartlo (High Dartlo in English). I was at the back of the group with our English guide Tom; as a graduate in Russian, he was able to converse with locals who were fluent in the language of their recent oppressors. A drunken shepherd invited us into his house for a vodka. We accepted. His hospitality flowed, but it seemed something wasn't quite right when Tom hinted to the drunk that we should leave. I found out later that the shepherd had threatened to get his gun and shoot us if we didn't stay and drink more of his wine. Not hospitality as we know it!

Lunch was taken at a house in Zemo Dartlo; coffee, Georgian style, being served on the terrace to finish. As we were leaving the man of the house arrived on horseback, well almost, as he was completely drunk. Much to his wife/sister's disgust she was ordered to get glasses in a way that would not be tolerated by an Englishwoman. He insisted we stay for vodka. This turned out to be neat alcohol, the local moonshine, best taken with water, or not at all. The drunk accompanied us during the descent to Dartlo, proving at least once that a drunk can fall off a horse without being injured.

After a thankfully dry night under canvas we de-camped and drove uphill to the start of the day's trek. It was cloudy and damp as our "flat" walk began. Despite not having a spirit level with me, I was certain that I wasn't walking on the flat; I suspect we climbed at least 2,000 feet in often swirling mist before making the summit. The descent was in sunshine for the most part, the scenery awe inspiring, the odd village dotting the otherwise green vertiginous slopes that led down to a mud-stained river.

After about eight hours of walking, followed by a lift in the truck across the mud-stained river, we arrived at our camp. No bathhouse to wash away the aches and pains of a hard day's hike; but there was copious moonshine vodka. This accompanied the alfresco dinner, and still flowed around the bonfire that lasted well into the night. A few locals turned up and joined us. The dreaded Tusheti accordion was spotted, an instrument that seemed capable of only one tune, the

Tusheti dirge. At first the tune was considered an interesting touch of local culture, but after the tenth repeat I began to look for the vodka bottle. Overnight a torrential storm flooded the campsite; fortunately, my tent was on relatively high ground. Someone else was not so lucky - she woke up swimming in three inches of water.

The Georgian crew decided that we should return post haste to Shtrolta a day early, due to the parlous state of the road, the additional rainfall adding to the risk of further shale landslides. While the campsite was packed up, a short trek was in order to the nearby village of Eleutra. A gentle stream on the path had turned into a raging torrent overnight and had to be crossed by a tree trunk fortuitously placed across the foaming water. This successfully negotiated, the next hurdle was a babbling brook further along the path that had turned into a wide river, albeit shallow enough to wade through with the help of my trekking pole.

The views on the climb to the Eleutra were obscured by rising air turning to mist, the humidity high from excessive rain; but the occasional glimpse of scenery, along with bushes of delectable wild raspberries, made the effort worthwhile. Eleutra contained no more than 20 houses, but still boasted a church. A local unlocked the building; its interior was a mixture of the religious and practical. A beautiful painted screen and ornate altar graced the inside, but also barrels of wine, the local cellar. The state of the paintings was poor, mainly, I guess, due to a missing window and the harsh climate.

Lunch was taken sitting on a balcony of one of the larger houses of the village. This contained a massive sofa-like bench, its timbers good for many a century; given its bulk, it could have come straight out of a 13th-century British castle.

The journey back to Shtrolta in the truck proved the wisdom of six-wheel drive, and also the precaution of a few extra Georgian hands for shovelling. Mini landslides made progress slow, but nothing the vehicle could not handle after a little spadework. The heavens opened again upon our return to Shtrolta, showing the decision to retreat from the campsite to have been a wise one.

The evening provided the chance for a slap-up Georgian meal. It was, after all, St Maria's Day, a big religious feast in Georgia. This, of course, had to be celebrated in style. Alas, this meant more accordion music, but also much wine and vigorous Georgian dancing.

Sunday dawned cloudy and misty, but dry. My knees told me to eschew the day's hike in favour of joining the crew, who were to take a look at the state of the road up to the Bani Pass, the only route out of

Tusheti. Part of the road was missing, swept away by the excessive rainfall of recent days. Driving out of Tusheti looked highly unlikely. We drove to Omalo, the only real town in the region, giving a lift to a contingent of the Georgian Army en route. Tbilisi was contacted on Tusheti's sole radio link with the outside world. Being a Sunday, Omalo was in relaxed mood, horsemen showing off their skills, and in one case his Kalashnikov. Yet more wine flowed back in Shtrolta that evening. Our chances of returning to Tbilisi to catch the flight home seemed slim.

At about midday on Monday, Tom returned from Omalo with the news that a helicopter would soon be on its way to pick us up. The Georgian Airforce helicopter, a twin turbo jet MTB capable of 380 kph, landed briefly in a cabbage patch next to Shtrolta, before flying off to a nearby ridge. The ground was too soft for a prolonged landing, so we were told to assemble, complete with luggage, in the field to await its return. The helicopter swung in, while the order to squat was given. The rush of wind made sense of this command, but didn't stop me from photographing our hasty entrance into the bowels of the helicopter. This was a powerful beast. It ascended with ease, the 30 or so passengers, many being locals who had hitched a ride, and sundry luggage, proving a lightweight load.

The climb through the valley of the Bani Pass was spectacular, the rotors seemingly skimming the edges of the mountain. Maria produced cups and enough vodka for drinks all round. The in-flight alcohol was consumed with much relish, and, surprise, surprise, another toast. The journey to Tbilisi had taken all of 30 minutes compared with a day and a half by road.

The last day was spent exploring Tbilisi, the once elegant capital of Georgia. After the slow pace of Tusheti, the streets of Tbilisi seemed frenetic with much traffic to be avoided, but at least, despite the pollution, there was 25% more oxygen to breathe. A combination of east and west, it veers towards Europe, but with Asian touches. A mixture of old churches, Soviet decaying architecture, ugly concrete blocks prominent on the horizon, but also the odd mosque and bathhouse.

Whatever happens to the Georgian economy and infrastructure, as long as it remains a country where hospitality is the national characteristic, a visit will always be a memorable experience.

The harbour in Plakias (photo: Helen Matthews)

News from the Front Line
Helen Matthews (1995)

I didn't think anything of it the first time it happened. I had just arrived in Plakias, on the southern coast of Crete, and was sitting outside a café, waiting for some much needed refreshment.

Then it happened again.

There was an explosively loud bang, which seemed to emanate from the jetty. A glance in that direction noted only a group of nonchalant-seeming locals, none of whom appeared to be armed.

Clearly it could not have been a bomb, and even the local hire cars seemed unlikely to backfire quite like that.

It was a day or so, and many sudden explosions, later that I finally realised what was going on. It was a few days before the Greek Orthodox Easter, which is celebrated, at least on Crete, as a cross between a religious festival and the English Guy Fawkes night.

The sound of fireworks grew more frequent, until, on the Saturday evening, the celebrations reached their culmination. Fireworks were even set off in the middle of the road.

I was fortunate enough to be taken to the church service in the nearby village of Mirthios, a couple of miles up the hillside. The church was packed, as was the tiny courtyard outside, where I was standing. Boys who had obviously never heard of the firework code stood on surrounding roofs and let off fireworks with great abandon throughout the service, but I was still not prepared for the finale.

At midnight, the priest came out into the courtyard with a candle, from which villagers (and the occasional tourist) lit candles which they had purchased earlier. It is supposed to be good luck if you can get home with the candle still alight. Having seen what happened next, I think it is probably good luck if you get home at all.

As the priest emerged, the church bells started to ring. An interesting technique was used for this - all the clappers had been tied together somehow, so that all four bells could be rung by pulling on one rope.

Meanwhile, back on the roofs, the fireworks reached a crescendo and an effigy of Judas was burnt. A German tourist next to me performed an interesting dance as he discovered that his hair was smouldering. The overall effect of smoke, flames, noise and explosions made me half expect to see Kate Adie.

Suddenly it was all over, and we returned to our hotel, where the proprietor offered us Easter biscuits, coloured hard boiled eggs and *metaxa* from his Easter table.

The timing of Greek Easter had not been one of my considerations when planning the trip. I chose April as I wanted to see the wild flowers at their best, but this was an experience I would not have liked to miss.

Meeting the Beer Woman
Patrick Cavanagh (2004)

My job takes me to many out-of-the-way places in Slovenia, Slovakia, Hungary and the Czech Republic. A few months ago I was headed for a beautiful little place called Ptuj in eastern Slovenia. There are no direct flights from Ireland to Slovenia, so I flew Aer Lingus to Vienna and took the Ljubljana train from there to a main rail junction at a little town called Prajersko. All the north-south and east-west rail services cross at this strategic junction.

I had about an hour to pass before the train for Ptuj, so I had a little wander around the place. Prajersko is a quiet little town whose rhythm is governed by the railway. I didn't want to admit that I arrived without a word of Slovenian, but I had taken the trouble to learn the words for "please" and "thank you" as these are the first words you must learn in any language if you are going to get on with people. You can have a great deal of fun getting people to help you to pronounce the local word for "thank you"!

Anybody who has been to central Europe during the summer will know that it can be very hot, and at a railway station there is very little protection from the sun, so I made it my business to find the bar and to look up the Slovenian word for beer.

I didn't have to look very hard for the name of the local beer as it was on the window - Läsko. So I asked the woman at the bar for "A Läsko, please", and got a big smile and a look of misunderstanding crossed her face. I knew from my wordbook that Läsko is pronounced something like Lesko. She and I had great fun teaching me the local correct pronunciation was something like "lee-yesk-uh." Let me say that Läsko/Lesko/Lee-yesk-uh is an excellent pilsner-type beer with a nice smooth taste that is very suited for the hot weather. A 500ml bottle costs €0.65 (£0.50). She recommended that I try the local brown beer called Bäron when I got to Ptuj, and to make sure it was served cold.

When I returned from Ptuj a few days later, to make the return journey to Vienna, the same lady was behind the bar, and she nicknamed me "Läsko," which I'm told is an honour, as tourists apparently are a pain in the neck complaining that there is nothing to do at Prajersko while they wait for their trains. (I called her "Läsko-dam" - Läsko-woman.) I now understand that in rural parts of the country, they divide tourists (and there are very few of them who venture any further than Ljubljana) into those who are "OK" and those who are not. Fortunately I fell into the "OK" category. It appears that many locals are extremely self-conscious of their poverty, and don't like to be reminded of it by criticism from tourists passing through.

Ptuj (pronounced something like put-twee) is a lovely little town straddling the river with an unpronounceable local name. It looks the sort of place that time forgot to change. There is a castle overlooking the town that was ancient when Christopher Columbus went across the Atlantic. A dark-haired tour guide called Maria Pop asked me, in her lovely blend of school English and German, if I knew a certain gentleman she fancied, who lived in Ireland. By a sheer fluke, it happened that I did; I was able to send her his address (after checking with him, on my return, that this was OK with him). It turned out the feeling is mutual, but he had lost her address shortly after arriving in Dublin when his apartment was robbed and vandalised.

In Ptuj castle they have a wonderful collection of ancient pianos and harpsichords, some of which are over 400 years old, and she played some traditional tunes on them. She allowed me to play a few simple tunes, all the time looking over her shoulder in case the supervisor was watching! It is incredible to be allowed to do something like that with a 400-year-old piano!

I mentioned that Ptuj is divided in two by the river. There are two bridges over the river - the original "old" bridge - now pedestrian only - and the new bridge that takes the cars and trucks away from the town.

Maria Pop had told me there is a strange "force" as she called it, on the other side of the new bridge right at the side of the river, and that if I was interested, I might go and feel it for myself. So I did, and it was very strange. Cross over the new bridge, with the railway to your left, turn right towards the old bridge, and you will feel a very strange "force" to your left. It makes your skin come out in goose pimples, and you feel your hair standing on end (I am almost bald, and keep the remaining hair cut short, so I don't know how it would affect long-haired people!) However I picked up a few dry leaves and dropped them, and they didn't seem affected, falling straight down. Maria Pop had told me that the force comes and goes, but she couldn't tell me if there was a regular cycle, or she thought it was connected to the phases of the Moon. When I got back to Ireland, a scientist friend suggested that it could be geothermal energy affecting a large body of iron in the ground making it strongly magnetic. There are hot springs about a kilometre away that have been used as thermal baths for hundreds of years, so that makes some sense, I suppose.

I went to a restaurant on the riverfront for dinner and asked for a Bäron (the brown beer that my friend "Läsko-dam" recommended to me), and enjoyed one of the nicest brown beers that I ever tasted. It compares very well with the excellent Orkney beers (including the Kirkwall beers such as "Skull Splitter") and the best Belgian and German brown beers. I mentioned this to the waiter.

I had happened to come to the restaurant whose brewery made Bäron on the side. The waiter wondered, would sir care to have a look around the brewery? All aspects of beer making were done on the premises; even the barley and hops were grown in surrounding fields, and the water came from a private spring 200 metres away on the side of the hill. Only the yeast was bought in - from two doors down the road! The barley was being roasted in a wood-burning oven and the guy in charge was checking that it was done just the right amount - too much or too little, and it would be unfit for Bäron beer (this at about 11pm). There was a lovely smell pervading the little brewery. I know a bit about the brewing industry, so I asked him some questions, such as where he got the water, how the yeast was used, and overall the way he made such a fine beer. It must have been 2am when I got back to the hotel, with a number of complimentary bottles of Bäron in my bag.

Overall, I found the Slovenians I met were friendly once they learned that I was not coming as a tourist to taunt them on their poor country. I got the impression that in Prajersko and Ptuj, the people were really interested in telling me their stories - there were some great stories - and listening to what I had to say. If their situation were different, I think they would be like their fellow Mediterranean cousins in Italy and Spain, and take a *mañana* view to life. But life in Slovenia is very hard, and it is a real struggle for most people to keep the wolf from the door.

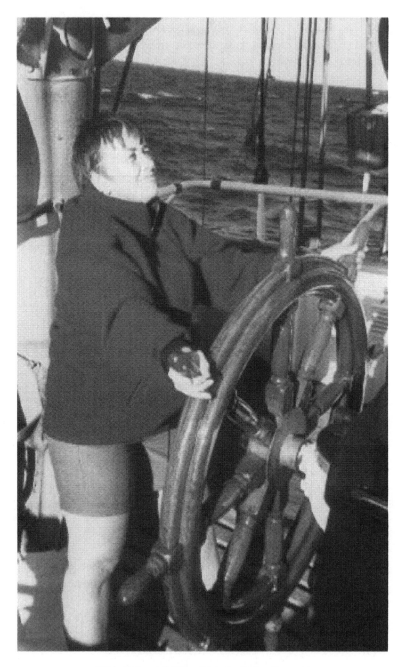

"All I ask is a tall ship..." (photo: Helen Krasner)

All I Ask is a Tall Ship
Helen Krasner (2001)

When I was around seven years old, back in the fifties, my burning ambition was to run away to sea. Despite discovering that I'd been born in the wrong century, and would have been the wrong gender in any case at that time, I never quite gave up this idea. So when in late 1999 I wanted to escape the hype of the Millennium celebrations, the Sail Training Association's Millennium Voyage to the Canaries seemed just the thing for me.

The plan was to sail to a number of the islands, the exact route depending upon wind, weather etc. We would have time to stop and visit parts of the Canaries which are off the usual tourist routes. As with all the Sail Training Association's trips, we would sail as the crew, doing everything involved in running a traditional sailing ship - sailing, cleaning, cooking, being on watch, and so on. It sounded very exciting. So despite the fact they'd virtually doubled their usual price - typically for Millennium trips, of course - I booked it without further thought.

A few days before Christmas we flew out to Santa Cruz de Tenerife, to board the ship which was to be our home - a definite misnomer - for the next two weeks. *Sir Winston Churchill*, one of two ships the Sail Training Association used for these voyages, was a three-masted schooner. To the uninitiated, this meant in essence that she had a huge assortment of sails with an even more enormous assortment of ropes to go with them.

I'd done quite a bit of dinghy sailing in the past, had a number of years windsurfing experience, and had spent a week on a flotilla sailing holiday in Turkey a few years previously. But I quickly discovered that this type of sailing was very different, in all sorts of ways.

For a start, there was the sheer scale of the operation. Raising and lowering sails required a large number of people, while changing direction, or "going about" was normally preceded by a call of "all hands on deck". At various times people had to "go aloft" to the crow's nest, while folding sails and coiling ropes seemed to be a never-ending task.

In the traditional manner, we 30 or so "trainees" slept down below on the "halfdeck", which was reached by a precarious system of ladders.

We were in two- and three-tier bunks, with a sheet-like attachment to tie ourselves in if necessary - you really don't want to fall out of bed in a strong wind. We were split into three watches - Fore, Main, and Mizzen, named after the three masts - and were "on watch" for different periods of the day and night in time-honoured naval fashion.

The actual workings of the watch system seemed at first to require a degree in maths to work out, but it really hardly mattered. It was very simple in practice - you slept when you got the chance, and got up when someone woke you, day or night. The watches rotated so that you were on different ones every day, a cunning system which seemed deliberately devised to completely mess up any kind of sleep cycle.

The novelty of this soon wore off, especially on the midnight to 4am watch, which I always found hardest. We generally lived on the halfdeck, which was where we slept, ate, showered, and relaxed on the odd occasions that we got the chance. The brochure had said we had separate facilities for men and women, but this didn't extend to sleeping areas; only loos and showers. But worries about where to dress and undress soon disappeared, since most people were soon too tired to notice or care.

We were actually a fairly motley crew, to say the least. Perhaps because of the cost, and the fact that many of us were Millennium escapees, most people tended to be single and professional. Overall we were aged between 17 and 69, with an average age of around 40. There were several teachers, an executive jet pilot, an advertising executive, and a sports science graduate - to name but a few. We also had a few young people who were being sponsored, plus a woman with learning difficulties who tried very hard but somehow always managed to get in everyone's way. We were led by a small permanent crew - captain, first officer, navigator, bosun and cook, plus three watch officers. The aim - shorn of all ideals - seemed to be that we did what the permanent crew told us, and learned as we sailed.

The Sail Training Association exists primarily to take young people to sea to broaden their horizons. The idea is that trainees learn to work as a team, and develop initiative, tolerance and other useful skills and attributes, while enjoying the whole sailing experience. The organisation has quite a number of adult voyages too, and really should have had experience in dealing with older people. However, I suspect that we were hardly a typical group. Which could explain why, early on, there began to be signs that the whole thing just wasn't going to live up to its lofty ideals. Indeed, it really wasn't working out well at all.

At first all of us were enthusiastic, motivated, willing to learn and to do as we were told. We had read the Sail Training Association's brochure, and were not expecting a holiday in the usual sense of the word. But soon it became clear that things were not as they should be. There were far too many conflicting instructions and general incompetence, and the plain lack of organisation on the ship began to annoy many people.

At first it wasn't clear whose fault it was. Suffering from an interrupted sleep pattern and intermittent seasickness, I even began to wonder if it was just me; perhaps I was too tired to think clearly. But gradually, as time went on and the confusion grew, people began to speak their minds, and those who had sailed on tall ships before began to voice their own doubts, based on a certain amount of experience.

"This isn't a happy ship," said one person - someone with a few voyages under his belt - after I began to voice complaints about the general incompetence. What did he mean exactly, I wondered. I began to look around me, to listen to what was actually happening, and it became clearer. Twice I saw the First Officer argue with the Captain over little things. Well, even I knew that on board ship the captain is virtually God, and must be treated as such. What was going on? I enquired further, and found out that most of the permanent crew had been called in at the last minute, owing to problems with sickness and personal commitments. So this bunch hadn't been meant to sail together in the first place. And the Captain was fortyish, female and extremely competent; the First Officer sixtyish, male and looking like he'd been passed over...I could draw my own conclusions.

Of course it wasn't all bad. Nothing, no amount of disorganisation or interpersonal bickering among the crew, could detract from the drama of sailing in the Canaries. It is an ideal way of seeing the islands as they really are, far from the madness of mass tourism. I will never forget being on watch at dawn and seeing the sun come up over the dramatically folded cliffs of El Hierro, the smallest and least visited of the islands. On Christmas Day, there was a meeting of tall ships in La Palma, another relatively unvisited island; we met other tall-ship sailors and compared notes on our respective voyages, personal differences forgotten in the general camaraderie.

It wasn't all work either; we had time to visit the islands, swim from the boat or isolated beaches, even sunbathe on deck occasionally. As for the actual sailing, I will long remember wrestling with the ship's wheel with all my strength, alone at night in a high wind while the rest of the watch handled the sails - such things are indeed as romantic as they sound. In fact, I thoroughly enjoyed the sailing, and seeing the Canaries from such a different angle. It was just the people who were the problem. One did get the feeling that the permanent crew would have been happier with a group of teenagers than the intelligent, well-educated, and as a result often stroppy bunch of adults they'd ended up with. We just did not take kindly to being told our bunks were "beginning to look like your rooms at home", by the First Officer. We objected when, during "Happy Hour" (ship cleaning), four people were sent to trip over each other below decks, doing a job that one could have done much more efficiently. We were willing to clean the decks, but we asked awkward questions such as why we had to do so in a force six wind with the boat heeling over quite dangerously.

I finally lost my temper completely when I was asked to do something, then told two minutes later by someone else that it was dangerous. "I do understand how you feel," said my watch officer, putting an arm comfortingly around me, as I spluttered with rage, almost unable to get the words out. Fine, I replied, but was he going to do anything about it? "Well, it's difficult..." In other words, no he wasn't.

New Year's Eve found us in Santa Cruz de Tenerife, enjoying a massive fireworks display put on for the benefit of the whole town. So much for avoiding the Millennium, I thought, though it was very different from being back home. We had a massive banquet and all thoroughly enjoyed ourselves. Christmas had been memorable too - a celebratory meal, a tour of La Palma, taking part in local celebrations. To be fair, the permanent crew did make every effort. Though somehow they seemed to make much more effort after my explosion, and on balance it was just too little, too late. And I can't understand how they could dare to charge the amount they did - well into four figures - then restrict wine to Christmas and New Year meals.

I arrived home a few days after New Year 2000, tanned and healthy looking, with bruises, calloused hands, and sun-bleached hair, one of the few people I know to have actually lost weight over Christmas and the Millennium. For several days, when I went to bed, the world rocked as though I was still at sea. I could sleep whenever necessary, and get up and dressed at any time of the day or night. It had been quite an experience. I found out that I love sailing, but not with forty other people. I found out that I don't suffer fools gladly, even highly qualified naval ones who are supposed to be obeyed at all cost.

And finally, I realised once and for all that I no longer want to run away to sea.

Day Trip to Albania
Philip Garrison (1998)

I was on a singles holiday in Corfu and one of the optional excursions on offer was a day trip to Albania travelling by boat from Corfu Town to the southern Albanian port of Sarande. As we approached Sarande by sea, the breathtaking ugliness of the place slowly became apparent. The town mainly comprised high rise concrete blocks of flats in an advanced state of dilapidation, against a backdrop of bleak and sinister mountains. As our boat pulled into the harbour, we were welcomed by a few small boys swimming alongside us, practising their English: "Throw me money!"

The bureaucratic hassles of entering the country, which included obtaining a visa for 30 US dollars or equivalent, had been dealt with during the crossing so there were no further delays here. On stepping ashore, we were herded on to some ancient coaches and driven through the town. What an experience: the few shops appeared filthy and window displays, where they existed, comprised such things as tractor engines, surely not an everyday purchase for the average Albanian. Piles of rubbish were everywhere, spiced up with the occasional dead car. There were few "live" cars and those which did exist were mainly BMWs and Mercedes, which presumably belonged to senior party officials. We were taken to a pleasant outdoor café in what was evidently the better side of town and, whilst we consumed our drinks, money changers converted our Greek *drachmas* into Albanian *leks*. Then it was back on the coach, where we were driven southwards out of town. The countryside was mountainous and had a certain stark beauty about it. The standard of the road was pretty poor, although I have experienced worse. Quite spectacularly out of place were isolated high-rise blocks of flats in the middle of nowhere, usually surrounded by untidy chicken runs. We eventually reached the objective of this drive, which was some Roman remains. This site was quite extensive and well-preserved, perhaps partly because of Albania's recent history of isolation from the outside world. After a guided tour, we were bussed back to Sarande and lunch.

This was acceptable and served in a restaurant which was clearly purpose-built to cater for tourists. Our desire to sample Albanian wine was frustrated as only Greek wine was on offer. After lunch, we had some free time to explore the town on our own. This was when the strangest experience of the day happened.

One of my three companions was Bill, an extrovert and likeable Glaswegian. "Let's have an adventure," he suggested, so we headed off down the street in search of local colour. We soon found a bar which looked reasonable. It was fairly full but we found a large round table to ourselves, sat down and ordered rakis. Raki is the local firewater, a colourless fluid that tastes like rocket fuel and has similar effects, as we discovered later - apparently it is not related to the Turkish aniseed drink of the same name. While ordering, Bill asked the waiter if he could tell us the Albanian word for "cheers". The waiter ignored us, presumably not understanding. But two men seated at the next table raised their glasses to us and shouted a word in Albanian. Thinking that these men were answering our question, we raised our glasses in return and loudly shouted the same word back, priding ourselves on our ability to promote international relations.

What happened next was that all the other customers in the bar, in unison, got up and left. There was nothing casual about their departure: it was an immediate mass exodus. We were stunned. I shall never know the meaning of the Albanian word we shouted, but I can only assume that it was one of the language's worst obscenities.

In due course we also left the bar - we were evidently bad for business. We wandered through the litter-mounded streets, dodging holes where drain covers were missing. We all agreed that our worst nightmare would be to miss the boat and be stranded here for the night. One of my well-travelled companions said it reminded her of the Bronx. Bill said it reminded him of certain parts of Glasgow. Eventually, we entered another bar, smaller than the first one, and empty when we arrived. However, after we had ordered our drinks, groups of men started wandering into the bar and hanging around rather threateningly. We soon decided it might be diplomatic - not to say life-prolonging - to leave. As we did so, I smiled an acknowledgement at what I took to be the proprietor. He shot me a look of such hatred that I jumped back in shock.

After this, we decided to return to the more tourist-friendly area at the quayside. Most of our fellow day-trippers were here, spending their remaining *leks* on various trinkets that free-marketeer stallholders were selling. In due course, we returned to the boat and then back to Greece.

If you go, my advice is: take care, stick with a group and...be careful what you say in bars.

Hope for Romania
Elizabeth Hicks (2004)

26 March. An Austrian autobahn, 5.30am. We have just pulled away from a service station car-park and snow has fallen while we were sleeping. The white-haired woman from Canterbury next to me is dozing with her mouth open, tired on the last leg of a week-long trip that she makes around eight times a year. This is a woman with a mission - Patty Baxter, one of the leading lights in Hope Romania, a registered charity that supports homes for the destitute in the town of Baia Mare, north-western Romania (see www.hoperomania.org).

This time I have been her co-driver, joining her in Frankfurt am Main at Sunday lunchtime. We navigate across Germany the way Germans do - not by motorway and junction numbers, but by the names of towns: Nürnberg, Regensburg, Passau, and then over the border and aiming for Vienna, Budapest... (The Hungarian border guards are obviously in EU-friendly mode now as they just take a quick look at our passports, ignoring the fact that the car is loaded up to the gunwales, and wave us through.) However, this is not a romantic tour of central European capitals, but a trip bringing clothes and Easter presents of chocs and "smellies" - but more importantly the money that is the lifeline for a home for 14 children, all but two of them teenagers.

We cross the mind-numbing flatness of Hungary but the motorway fizzles out after Budapest and we crawl our way via Debrecen (where signposts are like gold dust) to the Romanian border on ordinary country roads, where overtaking the numerous small lorries is impeded by our right-hand-drive car. The Hungarians have no such difficulties and charge along as if they were still Magyar horsemen, swerving and darting across the carriageway. Too risky, we think - which is confirmed by the accidents we encounter on the return trip three days later.

Entry into Romania is also simple - for the first time ever, according to my companion, who has been doing this run for 13 years now. With a relatively low (but increasing) rate of car ownership, you still see plenty of horse-drawn carts on the roads. And the roads themselves have plenty of potholes, some a foot deep. The last stretch of our journey, from the border to Baia Mare ("Big Mine"), is the most drawn out. In the villages the road is lined with the modest bungalows found in many eastern European countries, but the soil is evidently poorer than that in Hungary. No fertile plain here, instead small gardens containing a few gnarled fruit trees or a handful of scratching chickens. Not much of the surrounding land is cultivated at all.

I have been on the road for 24 hours by the time we are greeted at the gates of "Casa Hope", and Patty has been travelling for nearly 36 hours. I have had no sleep and try to be as bright as the children and their adoptive mother, who are desperately pleased to see us. Patty bought the house 13 years ago using a bequest from her mother and has since devoted herself to raising funds, first to renovate it, and then to run it as a home for children who had no other chance of leading a normal life. Most have been there for several years and they are growing up together as brothers and sisters. Mama is a sizeable Romanian schoolteacher named Doina, who combines unswerving practicality with mothering the youngsters, giving them love and security. Some of these children were abandoned, while others were brought here by their parents, too poor to look after them. In some cases the parents are either in prison or dead. Some of the children are disturbed, but all have a stable and loving permanent home.

This is not about handouts. It's real grass roots stuff. Doina and her husband (who is working in a different town at the moment, so I don't get to meet him) run their family in the Romanian way, with all its members integrated into Romanian society (unlike some inappropriate schemes whose orphanages look like palaces - they stick out like a sore thumb and seriously, is a spiral staircase suitable for handicapped children...?) The children attend a variety of vocational and other secondary schools, go to the disco, put pictures up on their bedroom walls, one has a pet guinea-pig... So teenagers tend to be the same anywhere, I think. If they weren't here they would be on the streets, in prison, or dead.

Baia Mare is a large mining town with a population of about 300,000. The streets are full of holes, the houses range from the spotless to the collapsing. There is obviously some civic pride, with a tidy town-centre whose shops offer brightly coloured goods suggesting prosperity, but the prices look Western to me. The old central square is being restored, but these historical buildings will need a lot of work. Some people around here have got money, but you don't have to look far to see a grim kind of poverty, such as in the rough concrete shell of what used to be a block of flats. No doors, few windows, no water or sanitation, just a shell - and yet it is inhabited. The ground in front is a sea of rubbish.

Against this, Casa Hope seems to be an oasis, but more importantly it is a family. They do not receive any money from the state, instead being supported by Patty's fundraising activities. They have to feed and clothe the children, maintain the house, etc. They employ a (talented) cook and a cleaner during the week, while at the weekends the children do the chores. They also pay a modest monthly honorarium to a local doctor, dentist and psychologist, who then make no extra charge for treating the children as necessary. On the edge of town, the cook's husband looks after the three pigs (I have never seen such sleek, healthy-looking pigs in my life) and a dozen chickens. I also spy some rows of onions growing beyond the animal pens. All these contribute to a varied, fresh, cheap diet.

Run by Romanians in a Romanian context, this project has earned a reputation for successful work with children who would otherwise have no opportunities in life, so now sometimes other groups ask Casa Hope for advice. ASOK, a Romanian charity run by local social workers, has approached the project, hoping to work with it. This charity wants to set up an advice centre for school-leavers and, unlike Casa Hope, has a chance of obtaining some EU funding. It's promising.

Hope Romania's activities are not limited to the home for the children. It has bought a small farm in Laschia, a village about 20 minutes by car from Baia Mare. We drive out there one sunny afternoon and park on the main road, and then have to cross a narrow footbridge with no sides except for a couple of strands of wire, and gaps between some of the boards. The river below looks rocky and cold, so I watch where I put my feet. In the village we collect the key from a neighbour. The farmhouse and barn have now been renovated, although more work is necessary on the house to prevent damage as the soil shifts, and a well has been sunk. And somewhere further out on another smallholding are Casa Hope's sheep and its cow.

Here the atmosphere is what strikes you - one of the most peaceful places in the world, something that touches the soul. The farmers in this area grow some crops such as maize and potatoes, and keep a few animals. The barns have large, attractively carved wooden doors and I fidget with my camera, also trying for a snap of the picturesque conical haystacks. It is hoped that this farm will provide a home and the chance of a fresh start for a prisoner (the stepfather of one of the children) due to be released this summer, and later on some of the children may move in when they leave home.

In addition, two derelict flats have been purchased in the town, and once they have been made habitable they will accommodate destitute mothers with their children. The builder is happy to press on with the work because he knows that Hope Romania is a reliable payer. Hopefully the flats will be ready in the summer. Another tiny, tiny bed-sit has already been repaired and furnished, and is now inhabited by one of the older Casa Hope children who has left home. The project used to run a bakery/bread kitchen, too, but they were cheated over the premises and it wasn't paying, so now that has been discontinued and the equipment sold. The proceeds from this will pay for some of the building work and clearing out the revolting sump of a cellar in the block where the destitute mothers will live.

By Thursday I have seen just about all they can show me except the local mountain scenery, but as it has been raining steadily for 24 hours we give up the idea and decide to leave after lunch instead of staying until supper. The journey unfolds in reverse: dreadful road surfaces, unguarded level crossings, modest queues at the borders but no fuss. In Hungary we are diverted across country because of an accident blocking the main road completely, and the rain turns to sleet. It doesn't stop, only the amount of precipitation varies. Close to Budapest the sleet is at its worst and, in the dark, I am sure this is the scariest motorway I have ever seen. Patty and I swap over as drivers frequently because of the strain, but we press on. Eventually we hole up for three or four hours to sleep after crossing the Austrian border and wake up in snow. But later, the German *autobahn* is fairly free and we can make up for lost time, gobbling up the kilometres as we pass the names of towns - Passau, Nürnberg, Frankfurt.

By midday I am home. The sun is shining and my head is humming with the experiences of the last five days. And I've got a numb bum from all that sitting.

Five Months in Poland
Bill Lindsley (1998)

The coach deposited me at eleven o'clock on a Sunday morning, as arranged, at a filling station on the motorway and left me quite alone. The school was supposed to send someone to meet me but, apart from three men who appeared to be stranded in a car on the other side of the motorway, there was no-one. Eventually, I went into the cash office in the filling station and found that the man in there spoke German well enough for us to communicate. He sold me a telephone card and was about to help me to call my contact number at the school, when the telephone rang. He answered it, asked me to wait and called to a man in the car on the other side of the motorway. While the second man spoke on the telephone in an agitated fashion, I mused on the lack of traffic on this important motorway on a Sunday morning. There seemed to be about one car a minute going along it. The man finally hung up the telephone and the garage attendant asked him if he would help me to call the number I had written down. With a rather bad grace, he took the paper, looked at it and immediately changed his attitude.

"Mr Lindsley?"

I agreed that I was that person. He then introduced himself as the Director of the school. He later confessed, through an interpreter, that although I had been the only other person at the filling station, it hadn't occurred to him that I could be a teacher. In addition to my case, I had a rucksack on my back - that, in his eyes, indicated that I was a "hippy". He had been phoning the school to ask them to find out why his English teacher had not arrived. He was very apologetic and bought me lunch in the only hotel in Złotoryja.

When I first accepted the invitation to go and teach English for a term as a volunteer in Złotoryja (near Wrocław), I thought that I would be doing the students a favour. For the previous two years, I had lectured to graduates and professors at the University in Wrocław during their summer holidays. It seemed a logical extension of this to go and teach children between the ages of fourteen and nineteen in a grammar school. In practice, it was not quite the same, however.

For the next five months, I was able to see Poland through my students' eyes as well as my own and that was quite fascinating. I was advised that normal teaching methods in Poland involved strict discipline and that, if I did not maintain it, I would have trouble. The students expected to arrive in my room immediately after the bell rang, to go to their places and to stand there until the ritual of my wishing them a good morning had been completed. Only then were they permitted to sit down. This was about the only ritual I maintained, because I wanted them to relax and enjoy their English lessons. I like to think that it worked in most cases and I certainly learned more about them that way.

Some of them decided that, as I wore a black coat, I must be a spy. On one occasion, when I asked them to write about their impressions of me, and what my life was like away from the school, I found that many of them thought that I belonged to the British or the Russian intelligence service. Others thought that I might have connections with the Mafia and that I was using the teaching work as a cover for something more sinister. The students do seem to be very concerned about the criminal gangs which have sprung up since the demise of Communism. During one lesson, I drew a rough map of the town on the blackboard and asked them to tell me how to get from one place to another. The idea was to make them give me directions such as "turn left" and "turn right". I made a serious mistake when I asked them to tell me how I could get to the cemetery. One of them laughingly produced a toy revolver and pointed it at me. At least, I hope it was a toy.

They were very inventive. One day, I asked them to write a letter of complaint about something they had bought. The most amusing letter complained about a toy rabbit that one boy had bought for his sister. It was very nice until the full moon, when it came to life, grew long teeth and bit his father in the throat, killing him. It then went on to bite his mother and brother, killing them, but when it bit his sister, it was poisoned. He asked then to send him a stronger toy rabbit as a replacement. Even the girls had a good laugh at that one.

I had a lot of free time and, before the winter started in earnest, with snow on the ground from November onwards, was accustomed to go for long walks in the countryside. There were numerous footpaths and the scenery was excellent. There are two extinct volcanoes close to the town and they were always worth a visit, with ever-changing colours and fascinating views of deer roaming wild.

On some of these trips, I was accompanied by one student, who took advantage of the opportunity to practise his English as well as being helpful. I was able to see the area through his eyes. He was the one who noticed the fox walking on the mountainside and he often pointed out items of particular interest, including one of only two known "basalt rose" rock formations. His enthusiasm was infectious and he delighted in showing me where the Polish equivalent of the boy scouts liked to have meetings during the summer. He had been a member and knew the area thoroughly. After the temperature had been below zero for several weeks, the branches of the trees were heavily laden with the most beautiful ice crystals and they were still in that condition when I left at the end of January.

It was wonderful to visit the villages in the area and to see people quite happily walking along the country roads, dogs running loose and enjoying themselves and chickens and other poultry just wandering across the roads at will. This was, of course, only possible because there were not many cars and it is clear that things are changing, but it was interesting to see the village roads blocked with people going to church on Sundays. At times like that, the cars simply had to wait. Back at the school, I asked the students what they thought about the increasing number of cars on the roads and tried to make them aware of some of the problems caused by the car culture, such as the need for by-passes and more and bigger roads. But their main desire was to have their own cars and to go everywhere in them. Many of them even went so far as to tell me that they did not approve of speed limits and other restrictions in towns. They wanted to be able to go where they liked as fast as they liked and only then would they feel that they had become equal to countries like England.

Another serious problem for me was the lack of employment opportunities. It was very depressing to realise that many girls saw their futures as going to the university, getting a degree and then getting married and having children. There was no apparent thought of a career in their minds. Of course, some had more positive ideas and wanted to become scientists or doctors. When it came to discussing the future with the boys, I found it even more depressing. There were so few opportunities that even the nineteen year olds had little motivation to learn anything. They could only see the possibility of doing manual work and there was no incentive to try for anything better. Many men are leaving the teaching profession because the pay is so low, several of my colleagues being expected to live on the equivalent of £80 per month. An electric razor would cost in the region of £50 in Złotoryja and that leaves very little for food. The school librarian got her degree while I was there and she told me that it would enable her to live more comfortably. Her wages would rise from £50 per month to £80. A factory worker could earn considerably more than that.

During the first week of my time in Poland, I was walking along a country road when I saw what appeared to be a dead body lying on the grass verge. I was quite concerned until I realised that it was someone who had imbibed rather too much alcohol. Until the snow arrived in November, I saw many more of them lying just where they had fallen. Nobody took much notice of them and they were left there to sober up.

Although it was often vodka which caused them to get into that state, there are other drinks which are even more potent. I was once shown one which was 98% proof. Before tasting it, I was advised to take a deep breath, swallow the whole measure and breathe out quickly. I took the deep breath, took a tiny sip of the liquid and certainly needed to breathe out quickly to stop the burning sensation. I declined any further offers and noted the label on the bottle. There were often empty bottles with the same label to be seen lying around in the places where drunks gathered. I was told that many men can see no future for themselves and turn to the bottle to escape for a while from the misery of their lives.

It is not all doom and gloom in Poland today. It is no easy task to change from a Communist economy into a capitalist economy and, during the transition, many people are suffering great hardship. But the future is getting brighter all the time. For me, it was a great experience and privilege to be able to teach some of the young ones and to see that, although some were unable to see the way ahead, many more had ambitious plans. I hope that, in some small way, I was able to help and to make them realise that English people are quite nice really.

A Literary Pilgrimage
Helen Matthews (2005)

The idea of a pilgrimage for religious reasons is centuries old. People wanted to see places mentioned in the scriptures for themselves, or to see or touch what they believed to be holy relics. Religious pilgrimages still take place, of course, but nowadays other journeys, such as those of crowds of Elvis fans to Graceland, seem to answer a similar need to tread in the footsteps of the revered, but without a religious dimension. The literary pilgrimage is another manifestation of this trend. More obvious examples would include the coachloads of tourists that descend on Stratford upon Avon in "Shakespeare's county", or upon the Yorkshire moors to see if the heights are indeed Wuthering.

One Easter, I paid a visit of my own to a perhaps rather less famous shrine, but one whose literary connections are in fact numerous. The town of Rye, in Sussex, is probably best known as one of the Cinque Ports (of which I now discover there are seven, but that's another story). It is also the thinly-disguised setting of the Mapp and Lucia series of books by E.F.Benson. I had long wished to visit Rye so that I could visualise Mapp, Lucia, Georgie, Major Benjy, Diva, Mr and Mrs Wyse and quaint Irene in their authentic habitat.

Benson lived in Lamb House, Rye, from 1919 until his death in 1940. For a few years he was joined by his brother, A.C.Benson, a Cambridge don who wrote the words to *Land of Hope and Glory*. He had first visited the house some years earlier, as the guest of the novelist Henry James, who lived there from 1897 until his death in 1916. The house is now owned by the National Trust, which clearly operates according to a hierarchy of perceived literary merit. No mention of Benson is made in the description of Lamb House in their general guide to properties, and he only merits a mention on one page of the guidebook, to James' six (plus several full-page photographs) despite the fact that he occupied it for longer, and actually used it, renamed Mallards, as a setting for four of his books - *Miss Mapp, Mapp and Lucia, Trouble for Lucia* and *Lucia's Progress*.

The townspeople of Rye take a rather different approach. The numerous bookshops prominently display copies of the Mapp and Lucia books and second-hand bookshops also stock an impressive range of his other novels, now out of print. Posters advertise guided tours of the Tilling locations. Henry James and other literary personalities associated with the local area, including Conrad Aiken, Joseph Conrad, H.G. Wells, G.K. Chesterton, Radclyffe Hall, Rumer Godden and Russell Thorndike, are also celebrated, but Benson is the clear winner. It was not initially clear to me whether this was because of the Rye setting of Benson's books, or because more visitors were interested in him than in James. However, the tourist information centre website settles the matter:

"Rye's most famous and best-loved author is probably E. F. Benson whose fictional town of Tilling is based on Rye - many locals say they can still recognise some of the characters! There is a walk around E. F. Benson's Rye during the summer on Wednesdays and some Saturdays. Enter the world where Capt Puffin and Major Benjy took the tram to play golf and Mapp spied on everyone's goings-on!"

Henry James is described in the website as "Rye's other literary celebrity". So the National Trust would appear to be in a minority.

James used to write in the Garden Room, a separate room built at right angles to the main house, during the summer months, moving inside to the Green Room upstairs during the winter. Benson, too, worked in the Garden Room, which he immortalised as the base from which Miss Mapp observed her neighbours. My first disappointment on seeing the house was the discovery that the Garden Room had been totally destroyed by a bomb in 1940. All that remained was a brick wall with a plaque. A small model of the Garden Room as it originally appeared was on display inside the house, along with a number of photographs, including one of the bomb damage in 1940, so it was at least possible to imagine how it would have looked. The house itself is occupied by a tenant and only three rooms and the garden are shown. A small room off the hall, recognisably the telephone room at Mallards, contains a small exhibition about James and Benson. One of the exhibits is an original letter from James to Benson, inviting him to spend the weekend at Lamb House.

On arrival in Rye, the first thing I discovered was the reason for Benson's choice of Tilling as a name for his fictional version. This became fairly evident as we crossed the river Tillingham to reach the town from the visitor car park. We walked up Mermaid Street - could this be the original of Tilling's Porpoise Street, where Mr Wyse (and the dentist) lived? From Lamb House we walked past the crooked chimney to the church, with the Norman Tower, and thence to the Land Gate. Canny Tilling artists always painted the chimney as slightly more crooked than it was in reality, just so that there should be no doubt that the crookedness was deliberate. Later, walking along the High Street, I saw a middle-aged woman shopping with a wicker basket. This was truly the Tilling of the books.

In some ways, Benson's life in Rye seems very similar to that of his heroines. Like them, he supported the Rye (or Tilling) hospital. But instead of making bandages or lending use of his car, he contributed to *A Cargo of Recipes*, a collection of Rye residents' favourites sold in aid of hospital funds. His contribution is not however Lucia's infamous speciality, Lobster à la Riseholme, that was the indirect cause of two ladies going to sea on an upturned kitchen table, but something rather more sinister:

"*Pancakes à la Borgia*

Small pieces of glass (any broken window will serve)
3 berries of deadly nightshade
¼ oz foxglove
Dessert spoon of arsenic…"

He goes on to add that it is important that the host declines the delicacy himself for reasons of dieting. Benson also served as Mayor of Rye for three years, a post which Lucia eventually managed to gain in Tilling. Apparently this was coincidental, and Benson initially tried to refuse the offer of the mayoralty as he was just about to publish *Lucia's Progress*, the book in which Lucia becomes mayor, and was worried that this might bring the office into disrepute. Lucia paid for the refurbishment of the Tilling church organ; Benson paid for two beautiful stained glass windows in Rye church, one in memory of his father, Edward White Benson, the Archbishop of Canterbury, and the other in memory of his brother A.C.Benson.

James and Benson were not the only writers to live in Rye. Radclyffe Hall was another famous resident and sometimes dined with Benson at Lamb House, shocking the servants by appearing in men's clothing. Her house in Watchbell Street was apparently the original of Taormina, the home of Benson's quaint Irene, the artist of advanced ideas and dubious sexuality. Rumer Godden was a later resident of Lamb House. Russell Thorndike's Dr Syn novels were set on Romney Marsh around Rye.

As a result of my trip to Rye I learned a lot more about the setting of the Mapp and Lucia books, and about their author. But was my visit really undertaken for the intellectual reason of discovering more about the author and his works, or was it in fact a manifestation of the age-old desire for pilgrimage?

Travel Images
By Derek Trillo

Detail of bronze door, Sagrada Familia basilica, Barcelona, Spain

Above: Children playing on football pitch, West Bank, Luxor, Egypt
Below: Street scene opposite sculptor Rodin's house/gallery in Paris

Blackpool beach

Colossi of Memnon, West Bank, Luxor, Egypt, taken from a hot-air balloon

Town and harbour of Positano, Italy

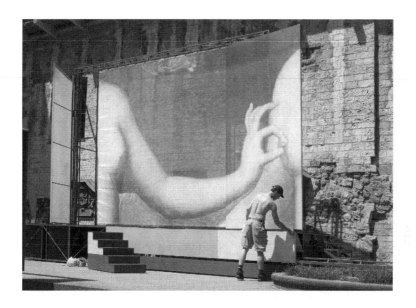

Above: *Workman constructing stage for opera performance, Prague Castle, Czech Republic* **Below**: *Traditional Czech musicians outside Prague Castle*

Tivoli Gardens, Copenhagen, Denmark

Above: *Detail of 10b Elizabetes Iela, architect Mikhail Eisenstein, Riga, Latvia*
Below: *Beach at Sorrento, Italy, viewed from a cliff-top*

The Americas

New York (photo: Philip Garrison)

Close Encounter
with Clotted Cream
Janet Baldwin (1999)

My husband has long wanted to visit the Arctic. I was not so sure, but here we were on an Adventure Expedition cruise in the Arctic. By our third day I was hooked. Illulissat and the Jakobshavn glacier were immediately placed on my list of wonders of the world. The sheer beauty of the ice and the majesty of the icebergs just took my breath away.

So having sailed uneventfully across the Davis Straits and, beginning to take Zodiac landings in our stride, we made our fourth or fifth on Charles Island.

Sun reflected off two small icebergs. In the bay, ice nestled against the rocks, a small attractive cove beckoned, our best island yet. Our guide ahead with the gun said head uphill, don't go into the valley to the right.

We headed happily up the hill, a scramble in hot sunshine. Flowers grew in every crevice. The valley to our right looked lovely, but probably a bit boggy, so the prospect of a good view was welcome. We saw our largest willow so far, no more than 5cm high but spread so wide within its sheltered spot. At one point we heard ravens calling from the valley.

My husband urged me higher with reports of a really lovely view. Just as I began to scramble up, a call came to return to the beach. The call was repeated from those immediately below; come down slowly to the beach. This was an expedition and we knew we had to obey. I scolded my husband as he and another man above him were still using their videos.

Making my way to the left, the way we had climbed up, I began to hurry a little, stopped to work out how to get over some deeply crevassed rock. Seeing people below beginning to panic a little but trying to keep calm, the words "Polar Bear" as if by telepathy began to murmur in the air.

There were two people ahead when I started down; they began to climb directly downwards. I knew I couldn't manage this on my own. Head right straight down - not the valley - came the call. I glanced up toward the valley, which was quite close now.

There, on a patch of light green tundra, was an enormous Polar Bear the colour of clotted cream.

I did not have time to think or look again. I headed down trusting someone would help me off the last six foot of hillside into the side valley - luckily, they did.

By the time we reached the beach, the hooters were going on the ship. We were told to make for the far side of the cove, to wait for a Zodiac to become available: one broke down; another was without a driver. We were all off the island, just as the fog came down and before the bear ventured over a small ridge behind which we were hiding.

I can still see the bear - reinforced by a clip from my husband's videoing companion, who panned into the valley from way above but sensibly kept quiet on the hill as he saw the bear. The bear himself does not seem to have noticed us; obviously intent on his own business, he made for the cove at the bottom of his own valley.

The guide who encountered the bear, having entered the valley to see why ravens were calling, was at one point within a hundred yards, worried that the bear would turn towards him and us before we evacuated the island. I had without realising been very close: not an encounter I will forget.

We saw another bear 25 miles out to sea swimming towards land. Our captain turned the ship around and we had a wonderful view - a much more relaxed close encounter.

One of our Buses is Missing
Margaret Firmston (2004)

Most of the passengers were asleep as we drew into the bus station at Chichicastenango, Guatemala, at 2am. The driver announced we would stay for 20 minutes. At last I could get off and find a ladies' loo. What a very strange place this turned out to be, however. All the bolts were on the outside of the doors!

Tentatively, I pushed a couple of doors as all were, of course, unbolted - after all, how do you reach an outside bolt from the inside of the door?! Each push resulted in voluble Spanish from the other side and the door was pushed violently shut.

"How do you tell which cubicles are occupied?" I asked a woman washing her hands; I was nervously glancing at my watch, fearing the driver might leave before 20 minutes were actually over. For answer, she bent right over beside the washbasins and peered underneath the line of cubicles to see where there were feet.

"This one is empty, *Señora*," she said.

Not much use - it had a big notice saying "out of order" on the door and a piece of frayed string tied across for good measure.

At least I knew they were all occupied and merely had to wait, hoping it wouldn't take too long. When I returned to where I had left the bus, there was an empty space.

No bus. It had vanished completely.

Now what? I tried to think logically. David, the guide, had seen me get off. He would tell the driver I was missing, wouldn't he? Unless of course he'd fallen asleep again? But I'd only been a few minutes, nothing like 20. Buses don't just vanish into thin air. Do they?

Quelling a feeling of rising panic I thought that, as I knew which town we were headed for and could speak Spanish, presumably I could get myself at least to the right place and possibly find the hotel (if the worst came to the worst) - couldn't I? However, the bus must be somewhere, surely?

119

"There was a bus here," I said to someone, aware even as I did so that this sounded pretty silly in a bus station. "Do you know where it is?"

"Oh yes; they've taken it away to wash it," came the reply.

To wash it? At 2.00am? With all the passengers on board?

"Oh yes," she nodded vigorously.

I tried someone else.

"They've driven it off to refuel it."

Slightly more believable.

"Is it coming back?"

"Oh yes; it'll be here soon."

At that moment, an unmistakable Australian voice, Greg from our group, said from behind me, "Oh thank God YOU are here, Margaret. Am I pleased to see you! It'll be all right now because you speak the language and can solve our problems."

Well, it was nice to be needed!

"I came out of the Gents," he continued, "And saw the bus being driven away. I chased after it and yelled at them and banged on the side of the bus, but they wouldn't let me on. David seemed to be arguing with the driver, but nobody took any notice. What's happened? What do we do now?"

I could easily picture Greg distraught and dashing after the bus with his long legs and probably waving his bush hat to attract attention. I told him what I had found out so far and, in view of Greg's unease, asked someone else what he knew about the missing bus.

"They've taken it to refuel it and wash the windscreen and it will be here soon."

That, at least, seemed to fit in nicely with the previous versions, so we waited. Greg was determined not to let me out of his sight as a useful interpreter, I was certainly quite happy to be chaperoned by a 6"2' Australian male.

A bus appeared and we stepped on, but where were our things? Where were the rest of the group...?

Wrong bus.

"You need to look at the number on the side to recognise your bus," helpfully explained a dumpy woman with a large basket at her feet. As the numbers on the sides of two nearby locked empty buses were the same as the one that had just arrived, this was distinctly unhelpful, but I did make a mental note to memorise at least part of a bus's number plate in future.

Another five minutes went by and Greg fidgeted nervously beside me, asking me what people around us were saying.

A man with a chicken under his arm asked if he was standing in the right place for the bus to Merida. Good. That was our destination too. At least someone else was expecting the same bus. The chicken seemed quite docile and unperturbed and nestled its head into the man's jacket.

The "wrong" bus left. More people came, with assorted bundles and bags and stood quietly.

Another bus. People stirred. Ah yes. A wet windscreen. There was David.

Greg greeted him volubly. David, however, had not been arguing with the driver about letting Greg on; he'd been trying to get off himself! Nevertheless, in that bus station there was a safety rule. Nobody could get on or off any bus anywhere except at the side where the official stop was. Desperate or not, that was the rule and rules were rules.

Everything is really very simple when you understand the local customs!

The image of Che Guevara still looms over Havana (photo: Glen Strachan)

Land of Contradictions
Glen Strachan (2001)

Cuba - the very name of that island nation evokes so many images, past and present. The casino days and the big game fishing of the Hemingway times merges with the dramatic fall of Batista. It was a memorable experience to stand at the window of his former Havana residence and look out on the view that would be the last sight Fulgencio Batista would ever have of his island before he was forced into exile on New Year's Day 1959.

My generation read the romantic accounts of the Christmas Day arrival on Cuba, in 1956, of the revolutionary Fidel Castro Ruz and his twelve disciples and, while little remains of the Batista story, the Museum of the Revolution spares no detail in chronicling the rise of Fidel and how he and Ernesto Guevara retrieved Cuba for the people.

It is intriguing to tour this Communist Holy of Holies - the Museum of the Revolution - and to discover that the entrance fee cannot be paid in local *pesos*. To see the relics of Fidel and Che's revolution, we had to pay in US Dollars. The irony of the cult of the US Dollar in present-day Cuba is not lost on the local people who are paid in the near-worthless *pesos*, while luxury goods like decent food, soap, toothpaste and cooking oil are only available in stores where the sole method of payment is in US dollars.

We came to Cuba with an open mind, expecting to find something of the revolutionary zeal that we always believed distinguished this country from the rest of the region, but we encountered a constant range of contradiction.

Hemingway's love of the macho lifestyle of the Cuba of his time is well known and the sensuous nature of this island race has long been attributed to its mix of Spanish and African people. Surprisingly, the prudish approach of Castro's Communist regime seems to have made little impression on the sexual climate of Cuba.

Today it remains the most free and easy sexual place that we have ever visited. I appreciate the tradition of sexy Cuba, but it is still a sad shock to see very young girls parading in the main streets in their underwear, hoping to earn a few of the coveted US dollars. The sad reality is that their parents often simply accept the inevitable and the dollars that these young women bring home often make life just that little bit more bearable for all the family.

In a rather unexpected echo of the East Germany of the 1970s, any contact that you have with local people during your stay will be quite closely monitored. I must emphasise that my wife Flora and I never felt remotely threatened, but on several occasions after we had quite innocent and indeed really casual conversations with local people, we were aware that they were being hassled.

The Cuban Stasi seems to be alive and well in downtown Havana. The main government concern appears to surround a belief that many/most Cubans would like to leave the country and there is something of a paranoia about escape plans being hatched. We had nothing quite that revolutionary in mind, hoping simply to hear some of the wonderful music for which Cuba is justifiably famous. We were quite successful in this respect, although many of the name artists who have recently found fame in Europe were actually out on tour.

Despite that, enough talented performers remain in Cuba and, although a number of Cuban ballet dancers and sportsmen have escaped to fame and fortune in the USA, the seemingly endless conveyor belt of talent is still on show in Havana. We watched an excellent *Madame Butterfly* on our last night in Cuba but, unfortunately, we had to leave before the last act as the performance started ninety minutes late. That mixture of excellence and woeful planning was typical of our experience in Havana.

Five-star hotels cost in line with Western prices (credit cards are welcome: pay in US dollars) and these hotels compare very well with anything that we have seen in other parts of the world. Our hotel was rather more modest in stars and cost but it was still well-sited and quite adequate.

Restaurant meals were not cheap by local standards, and were broadly in line with prices in the US resorts. Not surprisingly, the food was good and one of our fondest memories of Havana was of a visit to the excellent Restaurant Floridita, one-time hangout of Papa Hemingway. As we were eating, the house band came round to each table and very good they were, too. Their leader Baz Trabane explained that his Trio Taicuba had been together since August 1945 and that they had often played for Papa H and his guests.

There were various photographs on the wall showing these old gents as younger men in the company of the legendary writer and hell-raiser. When they learned that my wife's name was Flora, they broke into their theme song, *Floridita*. Old they were - slick they were - well tipped they were. That was a grand evening!

Cuba is an interesting island with Havana a fascinating city in so many ways. I have recently spoken to several other people who have lately visited the country and it is significant that each one has cited a different aspect of the island. This really is a place to visit and draw your own conclusions. It is unique and its political system is most unlike any other in the region. Cuban art is entering a period of fashion and of course the Buena Vista Social Club and a host of similar records have established some of the great old stars of Cuban music on the world stage.

The cigar is obviously a major factor in Cuba's fragile economy and a visit to a cigar factory should be interesting - even to the non-smoker. Maybe the oddest memory of our visit was the sight of rows of workers sitting in classroom fashion, hand-rolling cigars, while on a podium at the front of the room, the reader sits on a high stool. To ease the boredom, the reader delivers a Spanish translation of the latest Grisham novel, while the rollers roll their fat cigars.

Employees are very poorly paid and use their private allocation of cigars to earn a few tourist dollars, so it is better for them if you buy their cigars rather than the ones on sale in the factory shops. On one level there is a fabulous vibe to Cuban life - especially in the balmy after-dark hours - but I must emphasise that it is possible to make a visit to Cuba that will render most of my foregoing observations irrelevant.

You can fly in on a 4/5-star package holiday in a beautiful resort complex where you will be looked after in grand style. Entertainment and authorised trips are available and in most months of the year you can happily lie pool-side, sipping a martini and enhancing your tan. On such a holiday, the political dimension will never intervene and your sanitised environment will even allow you to watch BBC International or any of the American Networks on the wide-screen television set in your room, as you relax after dinner. From your window you will be able to see some of the locals sleeping in boxes but, even in these ethical days, you could probably do the same thing in London.

Cuba gave us much to think about and it was interesting to see places such as the Bay of Pigs which, like much of Vietnam, became familiar during times of conflict in years gone by. We left Vietnam with a feeling of joy for the future of that country - now in recovery mode - and we hope to return there one day. We left Cuba with much less confidence in the future of its people.

There is a sense of crumbling grandeur in the buildings and the feeling that a leadership that started in such a fervour of idealism has degenerated into a Batista-style milking of its people.

More importantly, it is quite a nice idea to dress simply (unless you take the 5-star option) and just travel home in a T-shirt and jeans, leaving most of your other clothes and shoes behind. No matter what your size, somebody will appreciate your cast-offs. Believe me, they need the clothing more than you ever should.

Glimpse of a Beautiful Stranger
Philip Garrison (2006)

The immigration officer at Newark Airport had no time for pleasantries. "Why are you here?" she asked me bluntly.

But she wasn't interested in my philosophy on the meaning of life, or even the underlying reasons behind my visit to New York. "Vacation" was clearly the right answer, and that's the answer I gave.

Had I met that immigration officer socially, perhaps in one of the coffee bars that adorn every Manhattan street corner, I might have been more expansive in my response. It was February 2002, and I would have said that I wanted to see for myself how the city was coping in the aftermath of the appalling events of September 11.

I might have added that New York is a city I find endlessly fascinating: I had visited New York, briefly, three times over the last two decades, and have always left wanting more - a bit like glimpsing a beautiful stranger across a crowded restaurant.

When I eventually hit the streets of Manhattan, I was struck by the almost overwhelming police presence - at least two officers on every street corner, and sometimes as many as six or eight. This could not be normal. Eventually, stressing that I was a foreign visitor, I asked one of them why the city was so full of cops. "The World Economic Forum is in town," was his rather stony reply. After the riots that had been sparked in Genoa by the World Economic Forum's presence in that Italian city, New York was taking no chances.

So the police were massed outside (and inside) branches of Starbucks, drinking coffee, bantering amongst themselves and hoping for some action. According to the local television news, they got their chance that evening, when they brutally put down a half-hearted demonstration outside the Waldorf-Astoria Hotel.

Thanks to the conference, personalities as diverse as Bono and Bill Gates were in town. I'd particularly have liked to have met Bill Gates - perhaps over a coffee in Starbucks under a glowering police presence - to discuss that problem I'm having with Microsoft Excel on my ageing PC.

Well, you've got to do it, haven't you? I'm referring to visiting Ground Zero, the site of the World Trade Center (1970 - 2001). Unfortunately, at that time you couldn't just stroll down to Lower Manhattan and take a look. A large area around the ill-fated office complex was still sealed off and surrounded by high fences. There was, however, a hastily-erected viewing platform of timber and plywood.

To gain access to this platform I walked half a mile to South Street Seaport, a gentrified, malled, dock area near Manhattan's southernmost tip, where I joined a long queue and was eventually issued with a ticket to the viewing platform at a specific time later that day. On arrival at the viewing platform at the appointed hour I had to join another long queue of excitable and emotional people. A female police officer built like a Sherman tank was growling at passers-by to keep moving. "There's no stopping here, folks!" The Berry family of Huntsville, Alabama told me that this was their first visit to "the North" - but they were finding New York "too fast" for them.

The viewing platform was an emotional place. Its untreated plywood walls were covered with hastily-scrawled messages of sympathy, peace and goodwill - and there was a Roll of Honor listing the names of the thousands who had died in the tragedy. It's difficult for me to say what Ground Zero looked like then, as we were herded on to (and off) the platform in groups of fifty people, and were given only a few minutes to gaze on the site. It looked like a large hole in the ground, full of portacabins and construction vehicles fussing around, the whole surrounded by hoardings emblazoned with the logos of major contractors.

Elsewhere in Manhattan, life seemed to go on much the same as it always had. News reports immediately after September 11 suggested that New Yorkers had suddenly become charming, but I was relieved to note that the famed New York gruffness of service in shops and restaurants had now returned. A newsagent in Greenwich Village seemed unaccountably affronted when I bought a magazine, but perhaps this is better than the indifference that often pervades such transactions in England.

The locals also regard a British accent as some sort of speech impediment; I was simultaneously amused and annoyed when an assistant in a drugstore reached for a feminine hygiene product when I asked if they sold phonecards (no, I couldn't work it out either!)

So you want to go to New York? Just go, and go now. I've been again, twice, since that post-9/11 visit, and I'm going again next month for yet another fix of this incredible city.

Two Brazilian Cameos
Piers Newberry (2003)

Part 1

São Paulo is not for the timid. My guidebook reserves a dozen pages to describe the varieties of thievery present in Brazil. Unfashionable are the ways of bash, snatch and scarper, rather thieves either act as Samaritans distracting tourists away from busy streets or in police costume they demand the payment of contrived fines. They mug in the Brazilian way, they mug with flair and imagination.

A huge, pugnacious man comes on television every night to front a programme called *City Alert,* in which traffic reports are interspersed with live video footage of criminals being arrested. The battle between right and wrong is intense; he roves up and down the studio floor like a peeved preacher and smacks his fist into his palm declaiming the perils and stupidity of crime; he points at the camera and speaks to them.

"We are out to get you," he says, but every night they are out and about and at it again.

Consequently on my arrival at the airport, with my heart racing and one foot thrust back to brace the cubicle door, I had the most tiringly gymnastic wee ever. It would have been better for me to have opened an account with HSBC prior to my departure; their cash point cards are commonly accepted and can be cancelled with a phone call. Erroneously I carried credit cards and the feeling of insecurity associated with losing them refused to dissipate throughout my trip. The card companies, heartlessly but sensibly, refuse to send out replacements and so a mugging would have entailed the end of my holiday.

São Paulo is a vast, unsatisfying city. I asked an inhabitant how he felt about it and a ten-minute tirade ensued. The pollution, the cars, the commuting times, the attitude...in fact, all factors which could be ascribed to a city were vilified and it was with a natural sense of relief that I found myself departing on a bus the day after my arrival. The terminus, like much of Brazil, is modern and efficient, but signs of the third world still show: the painfully thin shoe-shine boys and the man whose best option was to set up a plywood home on a motorway reservation.

The suburbs of São Paulo break away to reveal lush green hills. They are ramshackle, hardly touched by architects; they are wild, protected and unlike Surrey. In fact the only point marring their beauty in my mind was a subliminal expectation of seeing Tarzan, or at least Jane, hanging out the washing.

The relief, however, was short-lived.

At Curitiba, due to a slight error in my *Lonely Planet* guide book, I found myself wandering down a deserted dual carriageway looking for a non-existent hotel.

A nervous wreck of a man came up to me and said in Brazilian Portuguese, "Money have gun." He pointed to a gun-like bulge under his jacket.

"I'm sorry," I said, "I don't speak Portuguese."

"Money have gun," he said in English.

I replied in English, "Sorry, I don't speak English."

A delicious confusion arose in his twitchy little face. I turned and walked away. My irreplaceable credit cards would be safe until the next time.

Part 2

There is little to get excited about in Curitiba unless you are a socialist anti-car campaigner. It is rich and dull and full of cars.

A trip to C&A was the high point of my visit. The store assistant greeted me as if I was brown and squishy and stuck to the bottom of his shoe. He looked at my slightly scruffy travel clothes and demanded to know what I was doing there. It was confusing until I later related the incident to a Brazilian who told me that C&A is very chic and very expensive. I nodded and diplomatically scratched my nose to hide my smile.

I was hungry, so I ate. Brazil has some of the best restaurants in the world, simply because most employ a *por kilo* system. This involves loading a plate from a buffet and then paying for exactly what you have taken according to its weight. Restaurants which do not run this system often provide a *plato freito*, a simple and usually healthy plate of food, which is instantly available. The meals are cheap, but for most travellers who visit an endless stream of restaurants and spend a lot of time wondering when - if - their food will ever arrive, it is the speed and convenience of the systems which are most welcome.

Later, I walked around the town and failed to get excited in several different ways. Many of the streets are arranged in a one way grid system. This unfortunately causes one block of buildings to look much the same as any other and so leaves the place sterilised and characterless. However, it was a memorable delight to leave Curitiba.

A stream train shooshed up to the platform and with me on board it rocked and rattled down towards the coast.

Weird sculptured pines rose above well-kept flat fields shrouded in a delicate mist. In time the sun lifted the veil and revealed lush meadows and herds of sleepy oxen. As the train continued to descend, the evergreens gave way to tropical vegetation, bizarre eucalyptus trees, curious flowers and cascades of creeper.

Streams ran alongside and underneath the tracks and where the sunlight broke through the canopy, dancing shafts of light set the water quivering with life.

At length we trundled into a long tunnel. Its end broke darkness to reveal a chasm. The wide river at its bottom narrowed by distance to a rivulet. Kilometre-high granite monoliths stood at its sides leaning at impossible angles.

All pretension was lost and jaws dropped. The passengers gave a sigh, heartfelt and in unison.

It was wonderful. I had come away and been enclosed by the normalcy of Brazil: McDonald's to yuppyism, traffic and pollution. Here at last was something I had come away for, a sight empty of all meaning and full of beauty, mind cleansing and soul filling, something at last to bring a smile to my face.

Gorging
Hedva Anbar (2000)

Rafting through the Grand Canyon will be fun, I said to myself one dismal London day. I had shining memories of rafting with friends on the Lehigh in Pennsylvania, of sun, flailing paddles, shouting and laughter; of trying to steer our inflatable vessel like a dodgem car round the rocks which jutted out from the shallow water, shedding inhibitions and years, shoving and splashing as though we were five years young again.

A month later I was shivering in bikini, short cotton pants, T-shirt, socks and sneakers on the Colorado. The rest of my clothes were in my duffel bag, inaccessible till we reached the camp site. I was on the first of a flotilla of four rafts, swollen neoprene rubber tubing hugging lightweight frames with built-in ice and storage compartments, which could be mistaken by a short-sighted onlooker for a shoal of sky-blue hippopotamuses.

Why hadn't anyone told me how cold and wet it would be? I was still flight-shocked. My muscles were still aching from cramped plane seats. Chuck, our oarsman, passed a flask round the half dozen passengers on the raft. Gulping apricot brandy I forgot my discomfort, but not for long.

At noon we stopped at a narrow beach. The crew conjured up trestle tables and a picnic of oven-fresh white and brown bread, iceberg lettuce, crunchy onions, ripe tomatoes, velvety olives, pickled cucumbers, meats, rich creamy tuna salad, crackers and cheese, a cornucopia of fruits. I was glad I'd come.

But not for long. The Colorado was terrifying, deep enough in places to cover a seven storey building, wider in places than a terrace of fifteen houses, and only a tad warmer than the inside of my fridge.

The murky water surged forward, licked the salt-spattered canyon walls, nuzzled rocks, sniffed at submerged boulders, spat at choppy riffles, bolted through rapids. When I was not hanging on to the ropes for dear life, I was sitting numb-bummed wondering whether my swollen feet would ever return to their former size and longing for the Lehigh.

At 5 o'clock the next morning London time - no wonder I was tired - we moored for the night at a sliver of beach. I joined a chain passing equipment, food and buckets of river water to the kitchen area where the crew were preparing dinner. I lugged my gear up the slope to a wind-sheltered spot, cleared away stones, pulled my tent out of its carrying bag, threaded the poles through the sleeves, drove the pegs into the sand.

I hadn't the strength to unpack or wash. How could I survive another 168 miles, nine more days, on the river?

The gong. I crawled to the dining area. For starters carrots and celery with blue cheese dip. Followed by tomato soup. Mmm. My limbs were beginning to revive, my eyes to focus.

Succulent steak, best I'd ever tasted. Baked potato, buttered sweet corn, runner beans. Cheesecake - the sort that sent my tummy into raptures. Strong coffee, bitter sweet with a delicious aroma, in the light of a skinny moon.

The next morning I dressed, queued for the porta-potty and packed the things I'd need during the day in self-sealing plastic bags in a riverproof metal box. I stuffed my sleeping bag and other belongings into garbage bags, stuffed the garbage bags into a blue neoprene duffel bag and buckled the straps, dismantled the tent, shook it free of sand, rolled it up, stuffed it into its carrying bag and hauled everything to the raft.

Huge diner breakfast. River-cooled orange juice, tongue scorching coffee and chocolate, oats, warm muffins baked by the crew while we were packing, grilled sausages, eggs sunny side up. On the Lehigh we had only sandwiches and a thermos.

It was still cold most of the time but the sun appeared at midday for a few hours. We imagined human and animal forms in the black crystalline schist veined with rose and ruby granite rising from the water; in the red limestone streaked with silver-grey asbestos and dark green serpentine; in the layers of terracotta and magenta shale and ivory limestone stained with iron oxide and gold sandstone.

At the rim, a mile above us, white limestone cuddled up to a Wedgewood sky decorated with meringue clouds.

For dinner, bean soup, guacamole, tacos. A birthday cake for Frankie with pink icing and candles. For the rest of the evening we sat in a circle on the sand, drinking margaritas mixed in a battery-driven electric blender.

The sun was blazing down all day long now. Chuck put up a yellow parasol to shade his straining back as he guided our boat past the sacred Hopi Salt Mines, down the 20-foot drop at Tanner Rapid, 25 feet at Unkar Rapid, 15 at Nevill's Rapid. We photographed the bighorn sheep which patrol the cliffs. Lunched on antipasti, minestrone, crespella and watermelon.

Hance descends 30 feet. Chuck planned his passage to avoid the hungry boulders and greedy holes. He rowed into the first wave. We rose on the water. A wave rushed towards us from the right. Chuck rowed parallel to it, then backed into the wave approaching surreptitiously from the left. He rested when we reached calm water, but not for long: Stockdolager and Grapevine would be equally treacherous.

I took my turn on one of the twin outrigger pontoons at the bow, clutching the air-filled horn with thighs and palms, bruising as my calves collided with the tins of beer and soft drinks in the net swinging in front of us.

We glided through calm water, rose to the crest of a wave, sank to the bottom of a trough, faced a concave mountain of water shuddering as it made ready to fall on top of us, rose to the crest in the nick of time. Shoulder-high barrel cacti watched from the shore. A golden eagle soared overhead.

For dinner, fried rice, barbecued spare ribs, stir-fried vegetables and water ices, followed by Trivial Pursuit - the US version - round a driftwood bonfire and toasted marshmallows.

The moon was bloated. So was I.

From sitting watching the towering canyon walls all day and the moon at night, my skin and hair were dry as pressed leaves, my fingernails broken, my breathing wheezy. I wanted freedom. I wanted wide open spaces where I could run, jump and dance. I wished I could quit. But there'd be no way out till we reached Whitmore Wash.

Even Chuck was apprehensive as we approached Crystal. But no-one was washed off the raft this time. After hot dogs and bagels with smoked salmon and creamcheese - eaten standing up because the beach was thronged with red ants - we picked our way through giant boulders to a side canyon, along a crescent river bed to a waterfall.

And a rainbow. Its multicoloured spun-silk threads fell like lace through the tumbling drops of water, arched like stained glass in front of the rock, fragmented in the pool at the foot of the waterfall, a breathtaking kaleidoscope of dreams, wishes, past, future, pains, joys. The magic rainbow I'd been looking for since I was five.

Whitmore Wash. Under a pregnant moon the crew produced a crate of champagne, pinned emblems of rats with oars for tails to our T-shirts and welcomed us with hugs to the fraternity of river rats.

Four planes and seven time zones later I was back in London, stiff, tired, and full to bursting with shining memories of gourmet meals and a magic rainbow.

Amazon Experience
Sally Bishop (2001)

I awoke to my first sight of the river. The first thing you notice is that the water is a very unusual chocolate-brown colour, caused by the reddish soil it carries downstream. The short bursts of torrential rain, which we experienced most days, stir up the mud. The red mud caked our shoes and stained anything it touched.

Some of the time we could see both banks of the river, even if in the distance, and it was fascinating just to sit on the deck and watch the scenery slide by. On this trip, the temperature was mostly in the high eighties. We were travelling through tropical rain forest so it rained for a short time almost every day. One minute the sun was shining and the next the rain was coming down in torrents. Sometimes, there was gentle rain. The amazing thing was that we never got soaked. Every time it rained, we were under cover!

My enduring memory will be of the very tall trees and palms growing along the banks of the Amazon. The deep green of their foliage contrasted beautifully with the brown river banks and water. In my notes, I read that these trees were mahogany, rubber, kapok and brazil nut. Mostly there was no sign of habitation. We were there at the start of the rainy season so, in a few weeks, the Amazon would begin to rise and flood the forest.

Occasionally a clearing in the forest came into view, where there were a few wooden houses all built on stilts ready for the flood. We saw fishermen in canoes nearby. Black vultures circled the trees. We noticed huge moths and blue dragonflies sunning themselves on deck. During the night lots of beetles, bugs and crickets settled on the ship but I didn't see one mosquito, which was very comforting.

On the sixth day, we had sailed 295 nautical miles from Santana and arrived at Santarém which is a large industrial town with a blue and white cathedral. Here, the Amazon is joined by a 15-mile-wide tributary called the Tapajós. As he prepared to bring *Arcadia* alongside the quay, the Captain came across a problem. A pile of timber (probably mahogany ready for export) was stacked up just where our gangway would reach. Within minutes, he had turned the ship right round so that we could disembark. We were going to set foot in Brazil at last.

137

There was gentle rain as the bus left the quay, taking us out of town to a small settlement in a jungle clearing. On arrival, we went on a short jungle trek to look at the trees and vegetation. Having seen them from a distance, we were now able to touch them. Then we explored the village. The wooden huts had open sides and thatched roofs made from palm fronds.

The natives were pleased to show us how they lived. In spite of warnings from the others who thought I'd never get it off, I was brave enough to smear red dye on my face to ward off the creepy-crawlies, as we were shown! The people were self-sufficient, eating fish and *manioc* flour, which they process themselves.

In one hut, a man was opening brazil nuts with his machete. I hadn't realised that the individual nuts grow in groups inside one big shell a bit larger than a coconut. When he cut it open, there were 22 nuts tightly packed inside like a three-dimensional jigsaw puzzle.

At his feet was a small boy of about three, who was cutting up bits and pieces with his own knife. He was enchanting, as were all the children we met. We noticed that they were very placid compared with children at home. The simple lifestyle seemed to suit them. Pineapples, breadfruit, bananas and melon were some of the fruits we tasted. We were shown piranhas and catfish ready for the cooking-pot. Meanwhile Grandpa was sitting in his hammock watching us.

Before we left, we saw the collecting of latex from the rubber trees. The bus then took us to an old-fashioned rubber factory and on to the vegetable market near the cathedral in Santarém. Around here were the first shops we had seen for days and so the hunt was on to find postcards to send home. We were disappointed (but not really surprised) to find only faded cards with curled edges. The same thing happened at all our riverside stops. Amazonia is not geared-up for tourism. How refreshing!

Next day, we sailed up the deepest part of the Amazon for about 45 minutes to Alter Do Chao, a large village on the Tapajós River where the white sandy beach overlooks an idyllic turquoise lagoon. This is a popular retreat for residents of Santarém. The exotic shore looks almost out of place yet comes as a delightful surprise on arrival. We explored on foot and were greeted by children selling bead necklaces. (I discovered afterwards that, as only about a dozen ocean liners visit Amazonia each year, the children had a day off school to see us.) Some were carrying their pets and I gasped when I saw a girl with her sloth, which was about the size of a cat. It was clinging on to her chest with its long claws.

An Amazon mother and child (photo: Sally Bishop)

We walked along the tree-lined square with its array of hammocks and local crafts, past the cream-painted church towards the Centre for the Preservation of Indigenous Art Culture and Sciences. This is a very interesting museum, which was opened in 1992. It has magnificent displays of masks, ceremonial clothing and other artefacts from most of the tribes of the Brazilian Amazon Basin. We saw evidence of 87 tribes, many of which are now extinct. There was nothing dull here.

I liked the two dancers in natural straw costumes, who looked like statues to begin with, then scared the life out of me when they leapt into action with a yell. During a short downpour, we bought eco-friendly souvenirs such as smooth wooden pots and boxes in the shop. As soon as it stopped raining, we walked to the lagoon and paddled, while nearby a woman and her child were doing the washing. The sun was now high in the sky and the pale sand was unbelievably hot, so we made for the shade of a deserted beach hut and got out our water-bottles. It was peaceful and very beautiful.

All next day, we were sailing upstream to Manaus, our furthest point on the Amazon. I could see the river bank from my bed in the cabin. The tall trees with the graceful silver branches were cecropia. There were also ceiba (kapok) and rubber trees, as well as tall palms.

White egrets showed up against the green. My little binoculars were useful on a trip like this. I joined a number of keen birdwatchers, some of whom had telescopes set up on deck. After the black clouds, down came the rain. Large insects like scorpions came to shelter on the deck. Then at 11.00am, we took on board two naval river pilots for the final stretch. We arrived at the floating dock at Manaus just after 6.00pm and stayed there overnight and all next day. To reach here, we had turned north-west from the Amazon into the River Negro at the Encontro das Aguas (Meeting of the Waters), where the two rivers run side by side for several miles without mingling. Seeing the two colours of the different rivers was spectacular.

We had sailed about 1,000 miles from the Atlantic and had reached the confluence of the Amazon and its tributary, the River Negro. (At this point, the Amazon is called the Solimoes.) Manaus is a big, commercial city and the state capital of Amazonas, which itself is almost twelve times the size of England. From here, ferries travel up and down transporting people for days on end. We could see passengers' hammocks on the open-sided decks as we passed these boats.

Next day, we left the ship on an all-day excursion by river-boat to Lake Januaury (correct spelling!) and Terra Nova Island. At first, we followed the two rivers and saw the colours running side by side. Carlos, our guide, filled two glasses, one from each river, and asked us to test the temperature. The Solimoes was much warmer than the Negro.

After about an hour, we transferred to a motorised canoe to go deep into the *igarapés*, the flooded overgrown tributaries in the Nature Reserve. Each canoe held only ten people, so we had a marvellous view of the water and the wildlife. Egrets, cranes and vultures were all around. We saw huge blue, apricot and yellow butterflies as well as red-and-black dragonflies. The sharper-eyed even had a glimpse of some pink dolphins. The large black and red moorhens stood out against the tall green grasses. It was very hot.

On our slow, quiet journey, we saw men and boys fishing with nets. They came up close to show us the piranha they had caught. Carlos grabbed a stick and held it near a piranha's mouth. Sure enough, the fish bit right through the stick! Children paddled their canoes alongside to show us their pet snakes and parrots. Leaving them behind, the canoe travelled very quietly so as not to disturb the wildlife.

Lunch was included on this trip and the canoe took us to a floating restaurant where we had a delicious buffet of regional dishes including piranha, manioc, pineapple, palm-fruit and baked bananas. Just outside the restaurant was a raised walkway, where we went to view the giant water-lilies *Victoria Regina* and the caymans swishing their tails just beneath. I think this was the hottest moment of the whole trip.

We then returned to the riverboat for the hour's ride to Terra Nova Island. On the way, a mighty storm blew up and we had to go below to shelter and to stabilise the boat. Five minutes before, we had been sunning ourselves on the top deck. The storm was much more frightening on this small craft than any we experienced on *Arcadia*. There was torrential rain for twenty minutes. It had stopped before we reached the island, but everywhere was very muddy.

When we landed, a new raised wooden walkway led us through sugar-cane and maize to a small village with six or seven thatched houses on stilts. There were some very pretty children here. One little girl brought her parakeet to show us. The free-range hens had very long legs and rather strange elongated necks: adapted for the floods, I couldn't help thinking.

Carlos took us round the village while his assistant, Francisco, made a bird out of a palm leaf, origami-style, for me to hang in my cabin. We saw cocoa pods growing amongst the rubber trees. Tomatoes, melons and marrows grew next to the tropical shrubs. This was the most delightful spot. With very muddy shoes, we went back to the boat. The Captain turned *Arcadia* round and we sailed away from Manaus.

By 6.30am next day, we had arrived at our final stopping place in Brazil, Boca Do Valerio (mouth of the Valerio). One of *Arcadia's* tenders took us from the ship through the marshland to the tiny jetty. This village is accessible only by river. About a hundred people live here and it was easy to see why they needed to build the houses on stilts. There was hardly any riverbank at all. The people here rely on slash-and-burn agriculture, hunting and fishing to exist.

We were invited to go into the school, which had one classroom with 21 seats, a blackboard and a few books. The church was well kept and welcoming. All the buildings had unglazed windows and, although we visited in the morning, the temperature was in the high eighties and climbing. The villagers here are ready for visitors and they had dressed up in native costumes. They all wanted to have their photos taken (for a small fee, of course). I bought a piece of local wood carving, which looks even more impressive now I've got it home.

As we waited for the ship's tender, it was fun to see the local children asking for ice-cold drinks from P&O's stall by the river. Soon after 2.00pm, *Arcadia* left Boca Do Valerio astern and continued down the Amazon on our way home.

Next day, we had our last look at the river and were treated to a beautiful equatorial sunset. While we were dining, we slipped unceremoniously out of the Amazon without realising it.

A Day I'll Never Forget
Margaret Firmston (2004)

No-one was surprised the hotel still had no water that morning. We had slept in as many thick clothes as possible, including woolly hats - no wonder frozen pipes had stopped the town's water supply. July is cold at 4,000 metres in Potosi, Bolivia. It was rumoured some parts of the town had their water restored - not ours.

We piled into a minibus for the trip to a silver mine. On the way we bought the customary presents for the miners - dynamite, detonators, fuses, etc., which anybody can buy freely, even children. We added cigarettes and large bags of coca leaves - illegal in England, but chewed constantly by miners to keep hunger pangs at bay.

We bumped our way up a rough mountain track, covered in fine dust - maybe the lack of a wash didn't matter! In the mining area we saw the "clinic". Most of us hunted through our bags to find plasters or antiseptic to add to the poor supply available.

We donned helmets and took a lamp burning a naked flame. The entrance to the mine was down a low-roofed, pitch-black tunnel with a steep gradient. The floor was uneven, with stones, rocks and pools of water - not easy, even in walking boots. If you wished you hadn't come, there was no turning back.

Ten minutes later, we came to a wide space at the end of the first level. Here was a shrine to a local god. The figure had a cigarette in its mouth and bottles and coca leaves strewn beside it, offerings given by miners for their protection. There was a stench of sulphur.

Some of us felt slightly queasy and decided against attempting the second level. Those who did, returned wishing they hadn't: narrow crevices to be crawled through, long sheer drops, all in utter blackness.

In the afternoon we drove to a naturally hot thermal pool. The water was so warm it was wonderful to have a swim - round the edge. A whirlpool made swimming across the middle dangerous.

The guide and the bus driver had bought a huge bag of potatoes while we were earlier getting presents for the miners. Now they made a fire and piled up some stones, leaving a hole in the centre where they poured the potatoes, covering the lot with the fine grey dust on the ground. Soon, our meal was perfectly cooked. Once the "oven" had been dismantled, finding the potatoes was quite an art; they were now the same colour as the earth and the stones. They were delicious, provided you didn't mind the odd bits of grit left behind in the process of peeling them. At least we could wash grubby hands in the pool.

We arrived at the bus station to get to La Paz - throngs of people with bundles. Bolivians accept resignedly and with little protest finding their seats taken or having to sit on the bus floor.

The women's skirts, their baskets of goods to sell and the child in the shawl on their back take up a lot of room on buses. If you buy from them, their purses are hidden under voluminous folds in their skirts; a bottled drink is quickly decanted into a plastic bag which you hold gathered round the straw.

To our surprise some of the road had tarmac, but this merely gave the driver an excuse to drive on whichever side of the road seemed the shortest between two points whenever he came to a bend. When the usual road reappeared, it once more felt like being in a high speed wheelbarrow.

There was one "comfort" stop - no loos, however - a nun lifted her skirts only yards from the bus, but the rest of us headed for a nearby wall. We spread ourselves at discreet intervals along its length; it was a very bright moonlit night.

Back into the bus until the early hours when we would have to stay on hard benches in La Paz bus station until the hotel was ready for us. Maybe a cold night in a hotel without water has some advantages after all!

Dodgy Dealings
Heather Wankling (2001)

Manaus is a hot and humid river port, with a huge opera house built incongruously at its centre. It is also the gateway to the jungle where we had lived for the last few days. We had built a shelter from palm leaves; swum with, then caught and eaten piranhas; watched plump pink river dolphins frolicking in the coolness of the late afternoon; tasted gum from the bubble gum tree, hearts cut fresh from palms and Brazil nut straight from the tree. The people who dwelt in the jungle were calm and gentle and willing to teach. From them we had learnt which plant will provide fresh drinking water from its stem, which gives best shelter from a tropical storm, and just how well the jungle is able to regenerate itself despite the best efforts of man to destroy it.

When the time came to move on from the jungle, it seemed natural to turn to the river for our route out of town. To my surprise our boat left Manaus pretty much on time, at 6.30 in the evening. We travelled west along the river, making steady progress and only stopping once to load up with supplies. A short while later I noticed the light of Manaus ahead of us - we had turned and were now cruising slowly back towards port.

Some distance from land, a small boat drew alongside us, and small bundles were passed swiftly and silently up on board our vessel. The transfer was completed in a few minutes, then we increased speed and continued on past the port, now heading east.

The captain stared fixedly ahead and pretended not to understand when we questioned him about what had gone on, but our fellow passengers told us that the boat had been picking up contraband to be transferred from duty-free Manaus to a port further up river.

A Brazilian traveller introduced himself and told me how he would much rather be flying. These river boats were always hitting logs and sinking - only a few months previously, 40 people had perished when their boat sank - and of course, even if you didn't go down with the boat, the river was teeming with caymans just waiting to get you!

Up at the front of the boat a *gringa* was arguing with a local about hammock space. The captain was called to sort out the problem and confirmed that the *gringa* had been there first. As the defeated man turned away with a scowl on his face, muttering, she confided in me that she'd be sleeping with one eye open in case he knifed her during the night. All in all, for the first couple of hours, I rather wished I had chosen to fly too!

Within a short time, though, the rhythm of the river had got to the passengers, relaxing them and massaging the tensions from their bodies. The *gringa* made her peace with her adversary, and the nervous Brazilian made his way to the bar and sank his fear along with a few bottles of the local beer.

Once we turned off the Amazon and on to a tributary, the Madeira, the banks were closer and we heard the chattering and howling of monkeys, saw brightly plumed birds, a fuzzy shape high in the trees which was a sleeping sloth, and once, the flash of colour of a toucan's wings. I felt as if I'd stepped into the pages of a Graham Greene novel.

Meals on board were taken in sittings around a small table, those who were first to eat being watched hungrily by those waiting, who would pounce at the first sign of a vacated seat. The food was good and plentiful - beans, rice, spaghetti and chicken - with crackers, jam and good strong coffee for breakfast. There were four showers on each deck, with water pumped straight from the river, and queues for the toilets meant that when I succumbed to the inevitable stomach upset, I gave up eating altogether - easier than being caught out on a crowded boat.

From time to time we'd pass small settlements on the banks, little more than a dozen people living sandwiched between the jungle and the river. The river permeated every aspect of their daily lives. They washed in it, drank from it and swam in it. It provided their food, their only means of transport and a place for their children to play and learn.

Hour after hour, the crew sat up ahead scouring the river for obstacles, at night with the aid of a flashlight. The river was never quiet, at times as full of traffic as a major road and clearly the hub of life in the area.

The time on board fell easily into a routine. Days were spent lying in the sun, watching the banks, reading, chatting, and daydreaming; evenings at the disco on the top deck where a group of "working girls" from Manaus would demonstrate how to dance the sensuous merengue, as we sipped *caipirinhas* and watched the constellations drift overhead.

At night, we lay cocooned in our hammocks, enjoying the feeling of cosy privacy, despite the fact that our nearest neighbour slept only six inches away. It was impossible to stay awake whilst being gently rocked by the movement of the boat.

Time passed, regulated no longer by clocks but by the rhythm of the river, ebbing and flowing in time to the heartbeat of the jungle through which it snaked. Because we had lost all track of time, our arrival was unexpected. Too soon we found that our journey was over. Four days and 600 miles after leaving Manaus, we pulled into Porto Velho, unstrung our hammocks, and were thrust once more into the heat and frenzy of a tropical port.

Middle East & Africa

Tomb of Queen Nefertari, Egypt (photo: Lynda Penhallow)

Iran - a Trip into History
Margaret Walker (2001)

For once, packing is easy - Islamic dress. So my friend Ann and I take ourselves off to a Muslim outfitters in Shepherd's Bush and emerge with a couple of all-enveloping robes and several headscarves, with which the obliging shoplady supplies little ornamental pins for securing them under the chin. For travelling, I wear a lightweight mac over trousers, a headscarf in the pocket for instant application on touching down in Teheran. Later, all the female participants make the day of a shopkeeper in Hamadãn by cleaning his shop out of *manteaux*, the long coat (usually black, navy or brown) worn by Iranian ladies as an alternative to the *chador*.

Teheran sits under a pall of pollution seen as a yellow cloud as you approach from the airport. It is pleasantly warm, but the sun is invisible. Most of the pollution comes from the vast number of vehicles, cars, buses, motorbikes, emitting uncontrolled fumes, but there are also tall chimneys sending out grey, black, yellow smoke to join the poisons threatening the health of the ever-increasing population.

Our hotel, the Laleh, is air-conditioned and sealed against the outside world, but we venture out to visit two splendid museums - the Carpet Museum just down the road, and the Reza Abbasi Museum, which holds many treasures of ancient Persian civilisations and a wonderful collection of Persian miniature paintings which repay long and close study for the detail of facial expression, clothing, plants and animals.

Crossing the road is an adventure - pedestrian crossings are ignored. The trick is to advance as a group and keep moving - drivers then weave their way around you. Amir, our Iranian guide, bravely waves the traffic down and we make it to the other side - and back. It has been decided that we will have dinner at a restaurant, to which our coach takes us down streets dimly lit by the fairy lights hanging outside shops and market stalls. There are very few street lights, except in the main roads.

Our first meal sets the standard for most of the meals that follow - barley soup, salad, yoghurt, meat or fish kebabs with plain and saffron

149

Netball (photo: Margaret Walker)

rice, slices of deliciously ripe, sweet melon. As the Islamic Republic is alcohol-free, we drink bottled water (tap water is safe in Iran, but heavily chlorinated), non-alcoholic beer (not recommended) or Coke. We are the only foreigners and are greeted with warmth and courtesy. Some Iranian families are eating here too, and stare with interest at this group of fifteen women and three men (including our guide) in our rather motley attempt at "Islamic dress". At this stage, trying to be correct, we wear the scarves well down on our foreheads. As time progresses, they slip further and further back, especially as we see Iranian women showing quite a lot of hair.

Leaving Teheran during the morning rush-hour, we experience more of the appalling pollution, and are enormously relieved, as we approach Quasvin, to emerge into clear skies and sunshine. Quasvin is a bustling town with busy shops and markets and we make our way down a narrow street to visit a 12th-century mosque whose blue tile-covered dome gleams against an equally blue sky. Sadly, we can't see more than the courtyard, because the mosque is in process of restoration. In the centre, a group of workmen attempt to rig up some sort of lighting - the wires trail rather worryingly in the central ornamental pool.

We walk to a little park, where two boys pose in front of a relief of Rustam (and I recognise with delight the hero of a Matthew Arnold poem studied many years ago), then we visit a shrine whose entrance verandah glitters with cut-glass decoration. Families come to talk to us, the children anxious to try out their English, the women pleased that we are trying to dress "appropriately".

We leave Quasvin and drive to Hamadãn. The landscape is arid and rocky, with little vegetation. We gradually come to realise that each town we visit is an oasis, and to understand the traditional Persian love of gardens with their flowers, fountains and rills, a glimpse of Paradise in a harsh land.

Hamadãn is the birthplace of the 11th-century doctor, Bou Ali, known in the West as Avicenna. A modern monument to his memory stands in the town centre. More interesting is the Jewish tomb of Esther and Mordecai, with its heavy granite door and Aramaic inscriptions. The custodian speaks good French.

Lastly, we visit the site of Ecbatana, capital of the Medes under Cyrus the Great, where excavations are going on. A stone lion, so battered as to be almost unrecognisable, is believed to be part of a monument erected to a much-mourned friend by Alexander the Great.

Courtyard scene (photo: Margaret Walker)

Nearby, a group of energetic schoolgirls play netball, wearing trousers, long tunics and medieval-looking black hoods.

An outing to Bisotun to view a famous relief of Darius is frustrating, because it is shrouded in scaffolding and plastic sheeting. But those at Tagh-e-Bostan, showing pre-Islamic kings with the deities Ahura Mazda and Mithras, are delightful, and we stand on a rocky outcrop overlooking the road to Iraq and contemplate the plain where Alexander's armies marched.

History is everywhere, and recent history too, for posters showing young soldiers killed in the Iraqi-Iranian war are prominent at every road junction and their graves are frequently pointed out to us. The young widows and families of these "martyrs" are a burden on the State and every encouragement is given for the women to re-marry, but with so many dead who is left for them?

A long desert drive, with some interesting diversions, including a nomad encampment, brings us to Eşfahán, where Ali, our driver, negotiates the rush-hour traffic jams. Eşfahán has been a magical name since primary school, where I first heard it, and it comes absolutely up to expectation, despite the fact that, owing to a conference of Islamic Ministers of Tourism, we tourists are turfed out of the best hotel in town!

The Meidun-e-Emam is a magnificent central square with fountains, surrounded by handicraft shops and a bazaar where we watch fabric printing and copper beating and we bargain for decorative boxes. The exquisite tile-work on the Emam and Lotfollah mosques is breathtaking. People are smiling and friendly. Waiting for friends as dusk falls, I am greeted by students anxious to discuss English literature. Together we recite Milton and quote extracts from Fitzgerald's translation of *Omar Khayyam*.

We visit the wonderfully restrained 11th-century Friday mosque, the Armenian Cathedral and, a short distance from the city, a synagogue with Esther's shrine and Jewish cemetery. Our evening entertainment includes wrestlers exercising at the *zurhan*, juggling, whirling and wielding vast Indian clubs.

There are elegant bridges with tea-houses under the arches and gardens with fairytale pavilions. But to remind us that not all is sweetness and light, the faces of Khameini and Khomeini gaze from huge posters, reminding us that rules may be relaxed but are not to be broken!

153

Another long drive across the desert and we picnic by Cyrus' tomb at Pasargadae, then on to Persepolis at sunset, when the evening shadows throw the processions of carved figures into even sharper relief.

A whole day is spent at this vast site, and another in Shīrāz to enjoy the rose gardens, quiet courtyards and picturesque bazaar. They say that if you're going to be ill in Iran, do it in Shīrāz, where the University Medical School is renowned. Sadly, one of our elderly Americans does fall ill. Paramedics arrive within five minutes of being summoned and whisk him off to hospital, where his wife reports both cleanliness and efficiency.

Our last major city is Yazd, where many of the population are practising Zoroastrians. The Towers of Silence, where their dead used to be exposed for vultures to pick clean the bones, are a feature of the landscape.

Another feature is the wind-towers, a traditional form of air-conditioning whereby hot air is drawn into a series of flues, cooled over water and circulated through the house. They make delicious sweets and cakes in Yazd. A lady carrying goodies to a funeral feast insists we sample her spun sugar confection.

For the flight back to Teheran, women enter by one door, men by another, but we all join up inside the airport. We are cheered to find the smog somewhat dispersed and the Alborz mountains visible - at least from the Northern suburbs where the Shah and his family had their homes and the aspiring middle-classes choose to live now. We take off our shoes to walk through the Shah's quite modest Green Palace with its French furniture and crystal chandeliers, and saunter with the townspeople in the pleasant park.

At dinner, our guide is joined by his wife. Despite his liberal views expressed during our tour, she is properly clad in black *manteau* and scarf, and allows him to decide what she should eat.

City of the World
Richard Kingston (2005)

As I walk along the broad Corniche on this warm October evening, a refreshing breeze blows from the American University that resides on the most picturesque campus in the region. The lively sea crashes against the rocks as lovers walk hand in hand and pause to kiss, while fishermen cast from their oversize rods into the darkness.

A small child confidently rides its tricycle as proud parents look on from a distance. Fishermen sit together alongside the balustrade, telling stories while their shining floats bob in the dark water and the *nargileh* they smoke reminds me of my own childhood. The sweet smell of apple-flavoured tobacco and the ever-present Arabic welcome *ahlen wa sahlen* encourages me to join them and we discuss the world, Lebanon, Beirut and of course its attractive and impeccably dressed ladies. A proud mother chaperones her daughter who is curiously dressed in white *hijab* and blue jeans and smiles as the daughter coyly blushes.

The fishermen offer me cigarettes and coffee, but I decline and continue my walk while the moon, almost full, glistens on the restless sea. A young girl glides silently past on roller-skates, seemingly in rhythm with the Arabic music that emanates from the many cafés and street vendors who display their produce; charcoal-grilled corn-on-the cob, *ka'ek* bread and *termos* beans.

The coffee-seller calls and, when he detects my accent, greets me in perfect English and, once he establishes from where I have come, changes to faultless Greek. He pauses to tell me how he sailed with a Greek line for thirty years before jumping ship in New York, where he stayed for three years before being expelled by the authorities.

An *arabiyeh* passes along the road, jingling like a Christmas sleigh; the driver proud, the horse seemingly oblivious to its surroundings as the passengers enjoy the evening air and the vibrancy that is Beirut.

Watch the birdie...(photo: Lynda Penhallow)

Egyptian Wonders
Lynda Penhallow (2003)

I had read Howard Carter's book of his discovery and seen the illustrations of the treasures from the tomb of Tutankhamun, but was totally unprepared for the sheer beauty of the colours. The Cairo Museum does not have air conditioning and it can be very warm inside. However, the treasures are kept in an air-conditioned gallery, so it is like being hit hard twice when you enter; once by the extremely cool air, once by the treasures themselves.

I took away vivid impressions of the artefacts and also of a very humorous incident when our museum guide got into competition with a French guide. Both guides were trying to give a talk about the museum and each seemed to think the other was standing in *her* place. They tried to shout each other into submission by giving the talk as loudly as possible, each in her own language, whilst exchanging ferocious looks. The two groups of tourists obviously enjoyed the unexpected entertainment and, coincidentally, we would meet up again further along on our travels for another very funny incident.

The bus took us to Memphis, ancient capital of Egypt, then to the step pyramid at Saqqara. We lunched at the Mena House Hotel where the dining room overlooks the Pyramids. After an excellent lunch we took a camel ride up to the pyramids. George, the poor camel allotted to me, was sitting and eating when he was given a sharp poke with a stick to make him get up. He complained loudly and spat his grass at me which was a good start because I was terrified of him, but had to get on his back! I was warned that I might find the Pyramids disappointing, because of their size and proximity to the suburbs of Cairo. However, that was not the case. The base stones of the Pyramids were almost as tall as me and I found them fascinating. There are all sorts of wheelers and dealers at the site, but Yasser was excellent at making sure we were not bothered too much. If you go around one side of the Pyramids facing away from Cairo towards the desert, it is easy to imagine how the site would have been in ancient times.

Very early on the morning of day four, we flew down to Aswân to join our cruise boat. Because of the fears of terrorism, the boat was much less than half full and there were only about 20 of us. The proposed holiday itinerary, by contrast, was very full and every effort was made to welcome us and make sure we all had an excellent holiday. The first evening, after we had settled into our cabins we enjoyed a sail on a *felucca*, and then had a reasonably early night as we were flying down to the Abu Simbel Temples the next morning.

The flight was great fun for two reasons. Yasser said that we needed to sit on the left of the plane if we wanted to see the temples as we flew down to the site. On arrival at Aswân airport, we found that the seating for the flight was not pre-allocated and sitting waiting to board the plane was the party we had encountered at the museum. It was obvious that our new friends from the museum had been told the same thing about the left hand side of the plane. What followed was hilarious. When the doors allowing access to the plane were finally opened, there was a skirmish across the tarmac to the plane and victory for our party! (I have to say that we did swap places with our friends on the way back so they had chance to see the temples from the air also.)

Secondly, the pilot flew the plane in the style of Biggles, and as we roared off down the desert, each of us feared for our lives. The plane was rocking from side to side, banking left and right and finally landed at what seemed a very high speed and a very strange angle. It remained a joke for the rest of the holiday and, on each flight we made after that, we looked to see how the plane approached the airport, hoping it would not be Biggles.

Abu Simbel is breathtaking. When you get off the plane there is a short walk from the air strip. You continue around a corner and suddenly the Temples are there, huge and magnificent. It is absolutely incredible that they were moved out of the reach of Lake Nasser and there is no sense of them being anywhere other than where they should be, until the end of the tour when you go behind the scenes and can see just how they have been reconstructed. I was amazed to see that the statues have British graffiti on them that were, in some cases, over 150 years old.

Every time we returned to the boat after an outing, the crew were there to meet us with cold drinks and flannels to refresh ourselves. The stewards also liked to play tricks with the clean towels and had perfected the art of what I can only describe as towel origami! We returned to our cabins to find towels shaped like animals and once a perfect little baby shape was laid out on the bed.

We had a ride in a horse-drawn carriage to have tea in the Old Cataract Hotel, where *Death on the Nile* was filmed and, next morning visited the Unfinished Obelisk and Philae Temple. We cruised from Aswân to Luxor, stopping to see the historical temples on the way. When we arrived at Luxor there were tanks and soldiers waiting on the riverside. We all made jokes about waking up to find machine-gun nests on the decks, but that was exactly what happened! During the night, without disturbing anyone, the soldiers went to work and the next morning there were machine guns attached to front and rear of the boat. From Luxor onwards, every time we got off the boat we had an armoured tank and two Jeeps with armed soldiers to escort us.

The people north of Luxor make their living from tourists and had been seriously affected by the lack of visitors. I was very worried about how we would be perceived by the locals because we must have seemed aggressive ourselves. The tank sounded its siren, clearing the road for our bus to pass, and the soldiers in the Jeeps waved their machine guns at everyone every time we went out. I was relieved that the locals came out to wave at us and shout their thanks to us for coming to Egypt.

In one town, they brought all the children out from school to wave. My husband's relatives had visited the area in previous years and advised us to take plenty of paper and pencils to give to the children. I added hair ribbons and beads for the girls and some cheap toy cars for the boys to my bag of goodies and all the fellow passengers were similarly prepared. The children were delighted and we had some memorable encounters with some, who rushed off to round up their friends to bring back to us: one child halted the tour bus by kneeling on the ground angelically pleading for a pencil. The driver let us off to give him paper and a pencil and he ran alongside the bus blowing kisses to us.

We visited some truly stunning places: temples and tombs with vivid wall paintings. The most beautiful tomb is that of Queen Nefertari and it is worth the extra it costs to visit because the colours are fresh and glowing inside. I was overawed with the size of everything we saw. Yasser took a picture of us standing next to a stone bird and we are very small against the bird. Then we took a photo of the same bird next to the temple and the bird is dwarfed. This gives some idea of the perspective which is missing in the photographs that you usually see. To walk in the Valley of the Kings was something I had dreamed of doing from childhood and when I had read Howard Carter's book, I never imagined that I would ever actually stand in the tomb of the boy king myself one day.

There was a very touching moment when we arrived at the site of the massacre at the Temple of Hapshepsut. I had not realised that the site was completely open and that there would have been nowhere for the tourists to hide to protect themselves or shelter from the terrorists. On the day we visited, there were men with machine guns sitting on camels all around the site and in the hills above. Our guide Yasser told us he was on the tour bus the day the shooting happened. He said that the stall holders who sell stone scarabs and souvenirs tried to help the tourists by throwing their carved stone goods at the gunmen. He had not unloaded his bus, but quickly turned and drove away, taking the tourists back to their boat. He said they were all offered the opportunity to be flown home, but the majority chose to stay. They were all deeply touched at the reaction of the Egyptians, who genuinely do not want the tourists harmed and who apologised wholeheartedly to them for the incident and the behaviour of the terrorists at every possible opportunity.

We finished our cruise with the fancy dress party, where everyone dressed as Egyptians. All the women had bought beautiful clothes from the various bazaars that we had visited and even all the men had made the effort and looked wonderful in their white *galabeas*. We enjoyed Egyptian music, dancing and food and the waiters sang for us.

We returned loaded with beautiful examples of the talent of the Egyptian craftsmen and women, but also with a different outlook on life. The memory of the beautiful, serene, dignified faces of the villagers we met will always stay with me and will remain thought-provoking.

We were given a free football when we bought a roll of film at a hotel shop in Luxor. Not wanting to carry it back to the UK, we waited until we saw a group of boys on the bank of the Nile and kicked it off the boat to them. The breeze caught it and the ball landed back in the Nile. The boys dived in the water and swam out to retrieve it, not without some difficulty, and took it back to the shore with great hilarity and lots of blowing of kisses. This started a bit of a debate amongst the fellow passengers about the wisdom of giving the boys the ball. Would it make them fight? We were of the opinion that you need more than one boy to play a game of football and from what we observed the boys knew that! I would like to think they are still having fun with it. So if anyone sailing up the Nile sees the replica World Cup football in action please let me know...

Race to Malindi
Richard Kingston (1990)

Many things impressed me on my recent trip to Kenya, not least of which was the journey on the overnight train from the coast through the national parks to Nairobi, but the thing which will always stick in my mind is what was to be a simple journey.

Buses ply along the coast road from Mombasa to Malindi and beyond to Lamu. We waited at a flooded village for only a few minutes when an ancient battered coach arrived. *Miranda* it said on the front, although the "conductor" assured us that it was going to Malindi and that if we didn't hurry, we would have to walk. It was only later that I realised that *Miranda* was the name of the bus and the reason for his haste had nothing to do with timetables (there aren't any) but a lot to do with pride, sport and profit. The bus operators make a lot of money from passengers who pay 25 shillings (about 70p) for the trip and you can cram about 60 into the bus!

We had been going for only a few minutes when through the torrential rain, I heard the drone of a 6 cylinder diesel engine fast approaching from behind and realised that this was no sedate urban service. The driver was swaying from side to side as the bus splashed its way through the potholes along this major highway and passengers jumped up and waved their fists at the screaming Nissan as it pulled alongside us.

The two coaches raced side by side until one had to give ground as another bus approached heading the other way. *Miranda* pulled back and the *Honey Dripper* shot past as chickens squawked and the conductor cursed and argued tactics with the driver. All was not lost though as the *Honey Dripper* had to slow down to take advantage of its favourable position to stop and pick up more passengers at the next village. Sure enough, the Nissan pulled in at the next stop and the *Miranda* shot past with the driver leaning on the horn as he overtook.

All seemed lost as the *Honey Dripper* reached the Voi river ferry first and gained a major advantage by taking the last place on the pontoon. Two pontoons cross as they traverse the Voi river and so it was only a few minutes before our driver was able to drive onto the other pontoon, while passengers bought grilled maize, toasted cashews and green coconuts with their tops sliced off to access the refreshing coconut milk.

Over the river, our conductor decided to head straight up the main road and give Kalifi a miss as all passengers waiting in the coastal town would have been picked up by our rival. Through the rain, we could just see the big Nissan turn out of the town onto the main road ahead. The long climb up the far side of the valley caused *Miranda* to complain but the *Honey Dripper*, for all its extra power, was heavier and now, weighed down by a full load of passengers, was struggling to gain momentum.

As we neared the summit, our driver got his chance and pulled out to pass the larger bus, while passengers and crew cheered. The rain lessened as we drove over the peak and, despite further stops, *Miranda* pulled into the dirty mud streets of off-season Malindi just as the sun came out and reached the bus station just ahead of the *Honey Dripper* and claimed her reward of a full complement of return passengers.

A day diving among the finest coral reefs in Africa would seem tedious after the morning's experience!

Brassières, Sherry and Lipstick
Celia Talbot (2002)

In 1955 I left Middlesbrough - a dismal post - on a cargo vessel, the *MV Baltistan*, to travel to join my husband in Basra. He told me that the sailor's name for the Persian Gulf was "the a*****e of the world", with Basra 40 miles up it. After a week in my bunk crossing the North Sea getting mother fixations on my Goanese steward, I woke up for the rest of the journey.

I vividly recall Port Said, with hundreds of goats all wearing leather brassières (to prevent the many children stealing their milk). I was taken ashore by a young cadet officer. I asked for cherry brandy, repeated several times by the waiter. The drink I received was a mixture of sherry and brandy. My good Yorkshire soul would not let me keep quiet when I saw my young host being short-changed. In those days, it would have been most impolite for me to pay my corner as I do now.

Later, I was taken ashore at Suez and entertained by a Lloyd's colleague of my husband's. The young clerk who took me on the launch was killed the following year, when Nasser had the Suez blocked by sinking many ships etc.

After the memorable experience of sailing through the Suez Canal, we called at Bahrain and later Kuwait. I recall a small dock, but there was the most incredible skyline (still there when Saddam Hussain attacked Kuwait).

I was taken ashore across two other vessels being lifted over bales of cargo, coils of rope and numerous ankle-breaking hazards. On the shore, I was greeted by a host from the oil company. Nearby stood a tall Arab with Tuareg head-dress and a large herd of jet-black sheep.

We were taken off the ship into the Persian Gulf on a raft being poled by a Kuwaiti young man in *djilabah*. We were given black sweet tea in small sherry glasses. When I handed mine back, it was refilled and handed, complete with my lipstick mark, to the captain.

A moment later, the man with the punt pole was in the water. He climbed back on board with the comment that his garment would soon dry. He did not possess another one.

Koutoubia Mosque, Marrakech, Morocco (photo: Helen Matthews)

Mud in your Eye
Heather Wankling (2004)

Everyone supposedly remembers where they were when they heard news of Kennedy's assassination. Being from a different generation, one of Thatcher's children, I recall vividly the moment I heard of her political demise. It was November 1990 and I was one of a small group sitting in the back of an ex-army truck, trundling through Spain, heading home after a six-month trip across Africa. To us, the news was yet another reminder that we were returning to our old way of life.

Over the past weeks, we had lived within our own small, slow-moving world, remote from life outside this one continent. The rumour of an impending Gulf war which we heard from a group of French soldiers in the Central African Republic seemed of less importance than news of border closures in Niger, riots in Nairobi or reports of sickness from fellow travellers.

For months the truck had been our home. We carried camping equipment, water and cooking utensils, and so at day's end we needed only to pull off the road, gather some firewood, and within a short time we had food, shelter and warmth. Even now the smell of woodsmoke on a warm evening takes me back to those African bush camps.

We were a group of diverse ages, nationalities and backgrounds: the engineer, who spent hours designing ways to overcome problems with the fuel pump; the chef who could somehow rustle up gourmet meals for 20 from the most basic ingredients; the joker - young, extrovert, and able to charm even the most world-weary; the wildlife expert; the gentle Australian giant; the innocent abroad. We were an eclectic mix but a strong camaraderie soon developed, engendered by a wealth of experiences shared and problems overcome.

The group first met up in Harare, from where we visited the Victoria Falls and rafted on the Zambezi river. In Botswana we travelled by dug-out canoe along the waterways of the Okovango delta, hippo-spotting, poled by a local whose glazed expression gave away his smoking habits. Sometimes, dropping exhausted into our tents, we would be lulled to sleep by the sound of distant drumming.

The East African game reserves teemed with elephants, giraffes and lions and we also saw rarer animals - rhino and cheetah. When we camped inside a reserve we kept a fire burning all night and our tents tightly zipped, lest a lone hyena mistake our sleeping bodies for carrion. We headed north through Tanzania, to the NgoroNgoro crater, an extinct volcano inhabited by an abundance of game and flocks of flamingoes.

Kilimanjaro brooded on the horizon as we crossed the border and made for Nairobi, where we stopped for a few nights in a hotel, taking time to scrub the accumulated layers of dirt from our bodies and clothes, and to collect our mail from *poste restante*. In this pleasant colonial city we visited Karen Blixen's house and went for a meal at a large restaurant, where we ate crocodile, zebra and antelope. Then it was time to turn westwards and start driving again.

In Kampala buildings still bore bullet holes from the years of unrest. Tourists to this "Pearl of Africa" were scarce, but beginning to return and occasional souvenirs were for sale. One night we camped by Lake Victoria and awoke to the sound of singing as the Ugandan army set off on an early morning hike, disturbing a warthog snuffling in the undergrowth nearby.

Zaïre, now called the Democratic Republic of the Congo, was once part of the Belgian Congo. Beneath the brightly coloured clothes and unusual hairstyles it was clear, from the reaction to our army truck, that memories of the country's turbulent past were still fresh.

Here we saw the strange okapi (created, it is said, with all the parts left over from other animals) and climbed into the Virungas to track a family of mountain gorillas. We trekked into the jungle to visit a small group of pygmies who, seeing white faces, assumed we were aid workers and asked for medicine for their chief, who had been bitten by a snake whilst hunting.

With the exception of a few major towns, all roads in the country were dirt tracks and, as the rains came, these rapidly became a quagmire from which we regularly had to dig the truck. In the humid atmosphere of the jungle washing did not dry easily and within a very short time everything and everyone had a muddy orange hue. Minor cuts soon became festering tropical sores and tempers began to fray as the hard-pushed truck suffered repeated breakdowns.

Eventually, after a month of mudholes, sickness and shortages of everything from flour to toilet rolls (and what seemed like an eternity of tinned sardine lunches), we crossed into the Central African Republic.

In need of some light relief, we went dancing with French soldiers in Bangui and, leaving the club late at night, found the streets busy with stalls selling hot drinks and snacks. We ordered fried-egg sandwiches made with crusty French bread and ate them at the roadside.

At the Atlantic coast of Nigeria we turned north once more, leaving behind the lush jungles and heading into arid regions where we were joined on the road by ponderous camels ridden by silent, turbanned tribesmen. In Agadez, Niger, we waited for some days for permission to cross into Algeria, which was delayed as a result of a political squabble with London. When permission was granted we moved quickly before the situation could change again, and started to make our way across the Sahara.

In the desert, more than before, we were thrown back on our own resources. Water was at a premium - the little we found was brackish - so for ten days none of us washed and we lived mainly on reconstituted dried packaged meals. These played havoc with our stomachs, weakened by sickness and grown accustomed to a diet of mainly fresh vegetables, fruit and fish. Among the dunes were hundreds of tiny shells which must have lain undisturbed for millennia, since the time when the area was a large lake.

Deserts are special places. To experience such total isolation, emptiness and perfect silence is rare indeed on this crowded planet. All too soon, once we left the desert, the trappings of civilisation began to appear, encroaching on our small, quiet world. We travelled on through the larger cities of Morocco, visiting the dye pits of Fez and the labyrinthine *souk* in Marrakech. In the Jemaa el Fna square at twilight, the smell of cooking offal filled the air. On then to the pretty coastal town of Essaouira and further north to Ceuta and the ferry to Spain.

On our last night in Africa we looked across the water at the bright lights on the Spanish coast and then turned back to pitch our tents facing south, to savour the experience of one final African camp.

Doorway, Palais La Bahia, Marrakech, Morocco (photo: Barry Needoff)

Expensive Freetown
Anne Rothwell (2005)

Sierra Leone is not the easiest place to travel to, but Marven had kept talking about going back there and showing the place to me. He had spent 18 months there during the war with the RAF in Coastal Command on the Sunderland Flying Boats, escorting the convoys as they sailed down the coast of West Africa, *en route* to the Far East. Despite the heat, humidity and insects in the mangrove swamps where they were moored; the fact that he'd caught malaria three times; the hunger when their supply ships were torpedoed, so they were reduced to surviving on mangoes, yams and tins of First World War bacon (all rind and water); he'd still taken a liking to the place and the people, whom they'd helped by building them Nissen-hut homes and curing some of their ills.

Flying to Freetown was a costly business, so we decided to book a package to The Gambia, giving us a base, so we could fly down to Freetown for three or four days. We wrote to Fourah Bay College, now the University of Sierra Leone, where they were billeted when they were ashore and received a reply, saying they'd be happy to see us. Having checked that entry permits were free on arrival for the British, we flew to The Gambia and duly got a reasonable flight to Freetown. On arrival, we changed just enough money for three nights' stay, to get a large wad of notes, then approached the Customs official. I should have known when I saw she was female that we'd have problems. From past experience, I've found that lady customs officers are the most hard-hearted breed in the world. She tried to take two-thirds of our money, saying it was for entry, and told us it would be the same amount when we left. Clearly this was corruption and we couldn't afford it. We argued, pleaded, showed her the letter from the College and I even tried a little put-on waterworks, but all to no avail. She told us we'd better get back on our plane before it left or wait 48 hours for the next one. So that was our brief foray into Sierra Leone.

The next day, we went to see the Sierra Leone consul in Banjul. His office was like a scene from a Graham Greene novel. The large African sat behind his empty desk and in the corner, a lopsided, rusty fridge whirred noisily, competing with the fan. No sympathy here: "You should have seen me before you went," he said. "They thought you were spies."

169

Travel Nostalgia

Photo: Neil Matthews

The Exchange
Alan Turner (2003)

French was my best subject at school and, as the School Certificate exam approached, the master suggested to my parents that perhaps I would benefit from an exchange scheme during the summer holidays. He provided details of an arrangement that could be set up through some Anglo-French organisation, which aimed to match pupils from similar families. It entailed a long questionnaire about accommodation, parents' occupation, pupil's standard, and so on.

It proved to be very efficient: my parents were shopkeepers in a small Worcestershire town, and I was linked with Jean Couralet from the *boulangerie* in a small town west of Paris. The idea was that the only real expense involved was the cost of a return ticket, as Jean would come to us for three weeks and then I would return with him to stay for three weeks with his family.

Uncle Percy, who lived in London, was volunteered to meet Jean at Victoria and put him on the train to Birmingham, where we would collect him. He was a year my senior, but very much more mature - his mother described him as *"père de famille"*, which seemed rather precocious for a 15-year-old (but there had been giggling at school about what the French were like). Apparently this just meant that he had no father and so was regarded as the head of the family.

Jean got on well with my pals, and we all improved our French as we went on almost daily cycling tours of the district within a radius of 15 miles or so. He was puzzled by the way our route invariably seemed planned to include a long rest near a railway line, especially the Lickey Bank which was only a 20-minute ride from home; train-spotting was a sport quite unknown to him, and he could not understand our enthusiasm on sighting one of the elegant recent Stanier designs storming up the long gradient. Some of the barrage balloons, now being sited as part of Birmingham's southern defences, could be discovered in fields a little further north. Then we would go to the Lickey Hills, overlooking the Austin motor works where they were producing Fairey Battle light bombers, and as each one came off the production line it was flown by the test pilot Alex Henshaw. We found a good vantage point to watch as he put it through its paces with thrilling aerobatics before approving its handover to the RAF.

The three weeks also flew, with swimming, sightseeing trips around the Midlands with my parents, and visiting relatives - especially Uncle Will who, by virtue of being a village innkeeper, had honorary shooting rights on local farms, and took us hunting rabbits (a regular part of our diet).

Then it was time for the changeover. Once again Uncle Percy was on hand in London; he took us on a tour of famous landmarks and then put us up for the night so that we could catch the Newhaven boat train next morning. We had what Jean described as a flat crossing to Dieppe, where my first impression of France was that although our train had an imposing-looking loco it uttered such an effeminate little whistle that it could hardly be taken seriously; no wonder French lads took no interest!

Dad had advised that we should take a taxi in Paris to transfer from Gare St Lazare to Montparnasse, and that really was exciting: I had never heard so much hornblowing, as our driver periodically slammed his brakes on and leaned out of the window to cuss a colleague / opponent and complain of the peril to which his important passengers had been exposed by the *imbécile* (or worse). We just missed our intended train - but it's an ill wind...we now had time to see something of Paris.

We left our luggage in safe custody and went by Métro to l'Etoile to see the Arc de Triomphe, and then feed at a pavement café in les Champs Elysées. We had hardly thought of eating during the day, and perhaps it was an empty stomach suddenly assailed by unaccustomed food which threatened an imminent upset; I was in urgent need of a toilet, and there did not seem to be any public ones - except the very public round stand-up gents' conveniences which were a famous feature of the Paris scene. So Jean negotiated with the café for the hire of a room upstairs, and I was soon feeling much better. Back at Montparnasse after another Métro trip, we retrieved our baggage and caught the train for Verneuil-sur-Avre, where we were met late at night by Maman and Odile, Jean's elder sister. Bed was very welcome after a long exciting day.

Jean lived with his mother and three sisters in a pleasant town-centre house, while his grand-parents lived at the bakery on the opposite side of the street, and we went over there for meals. After many years of an invariable English breakfast of bacon and egg, bread and marmalade, and a cup of tea, the first *petit déjeuner* was a real culture shock: a very large basin of coffee (consumed with a small spoon), the freshest possible *croissants* straight from the adjoining bakery, and *confiture* eaten with a spoon, thereby not spoiling the delicious flavour of the bread.

I was taken for a walk to get my bearings: not difficult because the town had three prominent towers well spaced out and of substantially different appearance. All I had to do was aim for la Madeleine, the tallest and most handsome, which stood beside the vast market square at the other end of our street. L'Avre, which flowed past Verneuil, had in the 12th century been the frontier between France and Normandie, so the town was defended (from the French!) by a broad moat, *les fossés*; the excavated earth had been piled alongside to form *les remparts*, whereon was an avenue of trees providing a very pleasant shady walk along *les promenades*. At intervals along *les fossés*, and also beside the Avre, stood open-sided wooden shacks; here women in long black skirts knelt at the water's edge punishing their laundry on ridged scrubbing boards.

Behind the house was a large garden, with many plum and pear trees, so we enjoyed plenty of fruit. "WC" painted on the door of a small building puzzled me; I asked one of Jean's sisters "qu'est-ce que double-vay say veut dire en français?" "Vatair closette," she giggled, but that was obviously a euphemism because I had peeped inside and was sure no *vatair* had been installed. Wooden boards covered a fragrant pit alongside, and on the wall hung some long-handled ladles with which its contents could be extracted - to the great benefit of *grand-père's* rhubarb and other crops. (OK, you can let go of your nose now.) The house had a proper indoor toilet, though I think it was fairly recent, and it was not available to the bakery workmen.

There was no bath on the premises, so armed with soap and towel I accompanied the children on their weekly visit to the public ones at the hospital, and for a fee of 4 francs one of the nuns who ran the establishment allocated me a private room with a bath of generous size.

A hydrant stood at the highest point in each street, and one morning each week they were all turned on to flush the gutters. The occupier of each property came out with a broom, to help any rubbish on its way clear of her premises, and presumably eventually into the Avre.

The weather was sunny and warm the whole time I was there, and ideal for cycling on the traffic-free unmetalled lanes in the surrounding area. Jean's school was a couple of kilometres out in the country, and had the benefit of an open-air *piscine*, so we often went there for a swim and splash about. The only time during the whole trip when I felt some anxiety was when I was told that the headmaster wished to meet me.

Jean had given me the impression that he was rather strict, but we had quite a pleasant chat in his study.

The one thing I really missed was the availability of soft drinks. Cycling with Jean and the girls, I was taken to call on various friends and relations around the district, and was always offered wine - usually served in ridiculous flat metal vessels about the size of a jam jar lid. And of course there was always a bottle on the table at mealtimes. To my unaccustomed palate it was horrid, as were the alternatives of beer and cider; I had never tasted wine before, and as a result of that experience I have never been tempted since. After suffering for a couple of days I sent an SOS home, pleading for a tin of lemonade powder to be sent. (Whatever happened to lemonade powder? Stirred into cold water it made a very refreshing drink.) My prayers were quickly answered: postal services were efficient at that time. The girls looked on with great interest as I mixed the stuff, and my thirst was assuaged; they had never seen or tasted anything like it before.

We went for excursions by car to Evreux, which has a fine cathedral, and to Dreux where an ornate hilltop chapel has tombs with effigies of the members of the Orléans family - though I was not really at an age to appreciate architectural magnificence. What did impress me was that the poplar-lined roads from one town to another ran absolutely dead straight for as much as ten kilometres. I found cycling along them awfully tedious, and much preferred the country tracks.

I often went with Jean or the girls delivering bread to customers near the town centre, so soon knew my way around. Twice a week I was also able to accompany Mme Couralet in her old Peugeot van when she served the more distant parts of the town: she just stopped periodically and sounded the horn until customers came out. But what I enjoyed most were the trips with *grand-père*, M. Durand, who had what I thought quite a posh Renault van for the rural deliveries, and we bounced along unmade tracks at an exciting speed. After I had helped load it up, we would set off before 8.00am on one of the country rounds, calling at farms and cottages. I tried to assist in finding the loaves that the customers asked for, but the weights were rather muddling. We (i.e. the staff of the business, of which I now considered myself a part) used kilos, whereas the country folk usually used *livres*, which were half-kilos, and so it was necessary to be sure which they meant.

The 4-kilo loaves were about three feet long and almost one foot wide, but one sort was even longer. Although we had plenty of 2-kilo loaves on the van, I was surprised that many customers asked for half of a 4-kilo one. I did not understand the reason at the time, but later guessed that they had worked out that the larger loaf had a lower ratio of crust to soft interior. The crunchy crusts that I was finding so scrumptious were, of course, very freshly baked, whereas our country customers were probably going to have to make them last for a week, by when they might not be so tender. We also sold a lot of *biscottes*, which I enjoyed too - they tasted rather like toasted brown bread. I thought it odd that when *grand-père* introduced me to customers and they asked "Est-il anglais?", he would say "Non, il est canadien." I could not understand at the time why my nationality should be denied in this way, and did not like to ask. Later, it occurred to me that *les anglais* were supposed to be incapable of speaking French, but it was well-known that many Canadians did, and that would pass as an explanation for my rather non-standard version of the language.

For several months the international situation had been deteriorating, with Hitler becoming more and more threatening in his speeches, particularly as regards Poland. English newspapers just seemed to mock him, with headlines like "It's that man again" (which soon provided the title for a radio comedy show). But in France he was no joking matter. People were becoming very nervy. In radio news bulletins the main theme was always "Monsieur Eetlair", but their papers seemed to devote more column-centimetres to air raid precautions in Britain than to their own. There was astonishment when Jean remarked that *les anglais* had all been issued with gas masks many months ago, whereas only a small number of Parisiens had been so fortunate.

On the railway, stations and signal boxes had their windows almost covered in blue paint, which was presumably complemented by orange lighting - one means of achieving blackout. All goods wagons had their capacities marked on the side: usually "Chevaux 8, Hommes 40", in readiness for troop movements. While we were in the house, ears were alert for *le tambour*: the town crier, who called attention by beating a drum instead of ringing a bell; he stationed himself at various points in the town to read proclamations, usually identifying the latest batch of reservists to be called up for the army. These were confirmed on posters which appeared almost daily, headed "Rappel Immédiat".

On Saturday 26 August the bakery's day workmen were mobilised (some who worked a night shift were still left) and I wrote home to say what an interesting time I was having helping out by hauling the trolleys of bread, straight from the ovens, and almost too hot to touch, from the bakehouse to the shop. With the girls helping serve customers in the shop, I was entrusted with making some of the deliveries in the town solo, and carried the long (unwrapped) loaves on my shoulders, rifle-fashion. We heard that, in some places, bakers with their workmen and vans were being "mobilised at home" to make bread for the government.

Mme. Durand was becoming increasingly pessimistic, bothered that I should have been sent home sooner, and now I was going to have to stay until the war was over...(Steady on, granny, it hasn't started yet!) But during the next few days, tensions increased rapidly. France and Britain had signed a treaty pledging that they would declare war on Germany if Poland were to be attacked. My Dad wrote on Tuesday 29th to say that, as Mum was worried, I should arrange to return a week early, on Monday 4 September, and he enclosed timetable details.

But mail was now being delayed - we heard that the government had taken control of the railways and that passengers were warned they might have to leave their train at any station to make way for troops. So when the letter arrived it was already Friday 1 September 1939: the day on which Monsieur Eetlair's invasion of Poland began. I replied immediately, to say that I might be delayed because, among the many rumours flying about, we had heard that boats from Dieppe had been closed to civilians, no trains were running via Paris where streets were being barricaded, and all Paris taxis had been commandeered, together with many private cars and lorries.

On Saturday, general mobilisation was declared in France, and a telegram from home, which had taken a day and a half, said "Return now". At the station a crowd of evacuee children who had travelled overnight from Paris were sleeping on their baggage, and we were told that after midnight there would be no more passenger trains at all. After frantic enquiries at the Mairie, Maman arranged for me to see M. le Maire, who signed and stamped a special travel permit for me. Verneuil was on a railway running east to Paris, but it was suggested that from l'Aigle, a town further west, there was a line to the north; perhaps I could get a train to Rouen, missing the capital, and maybe another train from there to Dieppe to try my luck at finding a boat still operating.

So Mme. Couralet drove me to l'Aigle, where there was a long train loaded with troops, camouflaged howitzers and other guns, but none that would get me to Dieppe before midnight. With ingenuity she managed to arrange for a hire car to take me the eighty kilometres to Rouen, and I found I had just an hour to spare before a train was due to leave for Dieppe.

This was very different from the express on which I had arrived in Paris less than two weeks earlier: it was on a rural branch line, and its cramped compartments were packed with country people and their luggage. At every station there were troops with steel helmets and fixed bayonets; they wore blue uniforms resembling the RAF, so I was puzzled why *l'Armée de l'Air* were guarding railway stations, but it seems that was the normal dress of *les poilus*. On arrival at Dieppe about 20.00, I enquired about sailings to Angleterre and was told that the next would be the last before the service was cancelled: S.S. Rouen would depart at 00.15, but no-one would be allowed to board before 22.15.

To pass the time after a meal at a dockside café I began to walk towards the end of the pier as it grew dark. Someone walked towards me and I stepped aside, but he moved the same way and shouted something I did not immediately understand; in the gloaming I could just make out the shape of a steel helmet and the glint of a bayonet - now I understood his challenge, and my French was really put to the test. Having satisfied him of my innocent intentions I returned to the quay, where over forty British tourist cars were lined up, awaiting their turn to be swung aboard by crane, but it was expected that many would be left behind.

In pitch darkness, apart from one green lamp at the end of the jetty, we sailed without lights, and the vessel was packed with people who had made long hurried journeys. They were sleeping all over the decks and it was difficult to find anywhere to sit. Then I joined some young Danes who had climbed on to one of the ship's lifeboats, which was covered by a tarpaulin that made a good hammock.

When I awoke, the sky in the direction of Dover was continually lit up by brilliant flashes, accompanied by an ominous rumbling sound; I was convinced that it was anti-aircraft fire and that a raid was already in progress, but found out later that it was only a distant thunderstorm. The only other light visible was the reassuring flash from Beachy Head lighthouse. As we neared Newhaven we were hailed by a tug and ordered to stop. It seemed that our ship had not displayed the appropriate identification and was refused permission to enter harbour.

There was a long argument between the tug man and our captain, who claimed that he knew nothing about any special signal. A morse message was flashed from the tug to a building on the hill; a few minutes later permission to enter was flashed back, our engines rumbled again and the ship groped its way into the harbour. Then came my first experience of the British blackout: total darkness apart from a dimmed hurricane lamp to mark the end of the gangway.

I slept all the way to London, and woke to find a city very different from that I had left a couple of weeks ago. Buildings everywhere were being surrounded with sandbags, more of which were being filled by teams of youngsters from sand dumped on the pavements, while air-raid wardens patrolled in steel helmets and hundreds of barrage balloons waved to and fro overhead. There was a long wait for a Birmingham train because all normal services were cancelled, the platforms were swarming with parties of schoolchildren being evacuated, and train-loads of them were leaving by the dozen. My main concern now was that, as a fourteen-year-old with a suitcase, I might be thought to have escaped from my school group and find myself directed to some distant part of the country.

We eventually steamed out of Euston, and the rest of the journey was an anticlimax. Relieved parents told me that war had been declared while I was en route. They had been desperate for news of my whereabouts, as they had heard nothing for days, and the telegram sent the previous day by Mme. Couralet to report my departure did not arrive until four days later.

Something in the Air...
Barry Needoff (2003)

The first holiday abroad I can remember must have been around 1963, at the time when package holidays were something of a novelty. It involved a long trek from my childhood home in Manchester to Luton Airport, for a night charter flight on an unknown airline (well, it wasn't BEA) to Rimini, and two weeks in an Adriatic seaside hotel.

The trek to Luton was quite slow and tedious - there were no great lengths of motorway in those days to make the journey even slower and more tedious. I remember little about the aircraft or the flight, but the first memory of somewhere foreign, as the aircraft door was opened, will always be with me.

It must have been the middle of the night, but it was warm and, mixed in with the kerosene smell of airports, there was that undefinable smell of something in the air. What was it? Herby, faintly tobacco, perhaps slightly sweet, perhaps slightly foul. I'd never quite smelled anything like it. Brought up in a city in the years before the Clean Air Act came in (and banished that all-pervasive smell of coal smoke) I wasn't used to the idea that the air could have a smell all of its own.

With daylight, bright new impressions piled on top of each other. It was so hot and sunny - whilst my parents fussed around me with sun-cream, the sand burned the soles of my feet. Even the pavements were hot - I had yet to get savvy and learn to walk in the shade! They did have the redeeming feature of water-melon vendors, who would offer slices of the reddest, juiciest and coolest melon I had ever tasted. Not like the melon we had at home!

The beaches seemed rather regimented, I thought. Row upon row of sun-loungers, chairs, tables and parasols - not like the random distribution (or chaos) of an English beach where you'd sit where you wanted. Despite the sun cream (it all came off in the sea!) I got quite sunburned, and this, combined with mosquito bites, made the humid nights unpleasant.

Some evenings there were firework displays, much better than anything I had seen at home. And I'm sure we did the usual tourist things like buying all the tacky souvenirs we could find. I remember a trip to San Marino where I indulged my childhood hobby of stamp collecting and helped to prevent the economy of this strange statelet from falling back down the mountain it was perched on.

Then there was the money. Italians used the £ symbol for Lire, so we thought it funny to see sweets for £50 a packet, shoes or clothes being sold for what looked like tens of thousands of pounds. I am sure we must have been given sweets or chewing gum as change because there was no small change in some of the shops.

I remember the food was certainly strange, but not unpleasant; breadsticks were fun (though impossible to butter) but I got a bit tired, I remember, of different kinds of pasta with every single meal. And fancy having bottled water with bubbles in - a bit like lemonade that wasn't.

But the ice cream! Being a child of the 1950s, for me the extent of English ice-cream exotica was Lyons Maid or Wall's "Neapolitan" - a bland, striped combination of strawberry, vanilla and chocolate. I had never heard of *Stracciatella* or *Tutti Frutti* or *Limone* before, far less tasted them. Wow!

I've been travelling pretty much ever since, on business, on package tours, independently, by air, sea, rail and car, and yes, the first thing I do when I arrive at my destination, is to see if I can still find that strange first smell of "foreign"... whatever it was.

La Belle Epoque
Lynn Hurton (2002)

My first ever foreign experience was of *la belle France* when I'd reached the grand old age of 16.

I'd begged my parents to allow me to go for two simple reasons: namely that I fancied one of the boys going (and yes, I did end up going out with him for a while) and also that I thought it'd be an enjoyable way to "revise" for my "O" Level French exam. Well, it certainly helped, although discussing bees, wasps and flies in my French oral bore no similarity whatsoever to the language I'd used, or at least tried to, for two weeks in the wilds of the Sarthe region.

I loved the ferry rides, laughed at friends who were seasick, discovered that my teachers were human after all, and arrived at *la Fête Bernard* a mere 14 hours after setting out from school.

My two weeks with a French family in the heart of the country were somewhat curtailed. Not by anything I'd done, but by the fact that Thérèse, my 17-year-old exchange partner, lived a mere 55 miles from the school. So, like her, I had to become a weekly boarder.

It was my first, and last, experience of boarding school. I remember endless soup, salad and sour apples, not to mention 40 beds per dormitory (single sex, of course) and only eight toilets per area. Add this to the six hand basins and four showers and you can see that it was "every girl for herself".

Two things I quickly learnt were endless swear words, especially when you were queuing and desperate, and to keep a stock of sweets on one's person. They made excellent bribes - it worked!

The weekends with the family - Mum, Dad and three girls - were very warm-hearted affairs. We talked, visited and did so much in a short space of time. So many memories remain with me:

The bedrooms next to the stables...

Being awoken by neighing horses at 4am...

The septic tank under the bedroom window...

The home-made cherry brandy and cider...

181

Huge old Aga range..

Six of us squashed into the French equivalent of a Mini...

A dorm midnight feast of nothing but sweets...

Fish on Good Friday...

The smelliest ever toilet in Vibraye (Sarthe)...

Lots of laughter...

Playing "*chevaux*" (French ludo)...

And discovering a lifelong love of France and the French.

I'd intended to be a maths teacher. In two weeks, my life was transformed. Languages became my new love. I chose them for "A" Levels and subsequently became a French and Spanish teacher. In my view, harder work, but more enjoyable than teaching maths. Yes, I have returned to the same place. I'm considered to be a member of their family and, yes, I still do love the cherry brandy and cider!

Before the Storm
Mike Cruickshank (2003)

I was an eight-year-old "married patch kid" traipsing from place to place at the whim of the Services. September 1955 saw us arrive at Nicosia airport. The first impression was of heat and dryness. Coming from the cool greenness of a late English summer, the heat was greater than anything I had experienced before. As a result of the long hot summer, the landscape was scorched to a dusty brown.

The first week was spent on the coast in Kyrenia which, with its Crusader castle, nestles at the foot of the Kyrenia Mountains on the north coast of Cyprus. Home, for the next year and a half, was to be the RAF base at Nicosia airport, which at the time was both military and civil. Going to school meant being bussed into the centre of Nicosia to buildings which had been commandeered for the purpose. Later we were to be moved to a brand-new school built on the base.

School hours in winter reflected the Monday to Friday 9 till 4 pattern in England. Because of the summer heat, the hours were rather different: 8 till lunch time, six days a week. As in England, playground crazes came and went. The only one missing was conkers, owing to the lack of horse chestnut trees. One plant which did grow prolifically had a bulbous onion-like root which, when cut open and rubbed on the skin, produced an itch. They were also used as ammunition in the resulting fights.

The long sunny afternoons were, for kids, an invitation to run wild. There was a whole new world to explore, from nearby unfinished buildings to caves in the surrounding countryside. The countryside, though arid and rocky, abounded with insects and reptiles I had never seen before. Anthills were two a penny, each with its column of foraging ants, larger than anything seen in England. Large spiders lay in wait in small holes in the ground. All that were visible from the surface were their gleaming eyes like two green pinpricks. Snakes were common, but as they were poisonous we avoided them as much as they avoided us. Lizards came in several sizes from the small shy gekko to the large, craggy (and, when cornered, vicious) rock lizard. Wild unkempt-looking shepherds would occasionally appear with their equally wild and unkempt-looking flocks. Despite appearances, both men and sheep were friendly souls.

Trips into town were a source of new wonders. Date palms, narrow mysterious alleyways, city walls thick enough to hold a parade ground on top, beggars, the red-and-white crescent flags flying in the streets of the Turkish Cypriot quarter, the sounds of alien languages; all were new and fascinating.

All this time, however the storm clouds had been gathering. There had been calls by the Greek Cypriots for union with Greece. They had been refused. The calls turned to action. A campaign of terror was started by EOKA. Bombs began to go off and shots were fired. Armed guards appeared on school buses and in the playground. The sight of armed troops became commonplace. Helicopter patrols also became a frequent sight. A large barbed-wire fence appeared around the married quarters. If it was meant to keep us kids in, it failed dismally. All this was seen initially as grown ups playing at cowboys and Indians.

Then a teacher left suddenly after her husband was gunned down in the street. Fear began to make itself felt. Trips to the seaside meant packing bucket, spade and sub-machine gun. The mysterious alleyways became menacing. Hitherto friendly shepherds were viewed with suspicion as potential spies, assassins and bomb throwers.

On top of all this, the Suez crisis flared up. A hutted radar camp was rapidly set up at the end of the road. A larger one further away from the soft target of the married quarters soon replaced this. The helicopters were joined in the air by squadrons of fighters and bombers preparing for a possible attack on Egypt. Speculation ran rife in the playground. Would we invade Egypt or would they invade us? In the event neither happened. The crisis died down as quickly as it had arisen. The Cypriot troubles festered on.

Life continued as before: an armed air of what had come to pass for normality on the surface with, for many, an undercurrent of fear. It was with a feeling of relief rather than sadness that I left Cyprus in mid-1957.

It was over a decade before I went abroad again, this time as a soldier posted to Germany. The posting was to Bergen-Höhne, within easy walking distance of the site of Belsen concentration camp, where the dead are buried in mass graves in their thousands and tens of thousands, and where birds and animals do not go.

It was many years later still before I could be persuaded to go overseas on holiday. I had seen Abroad and found it flawed.

Long Day's Journey...
Joy Toperoff (2003)

1987: Woken by the alarm. It's only ten past four! Oh, of course, we're off to Boulogne. Trundle my shopping trolley through the dark, through the rain, through empty streets to pick-up-stop number two, in front of Bejam's, Swiss Cottage.

Figures emerge from cars and houses. Just before five the coach arrives with the passengers it picked up at Finsbury Park. Women from a local tenants' organisation fill the back seats. We choose seats at the front. Clive and Hilary have brought three-month-old Angus with them. Rupert broke his glasses on the way here and can hardly see. Dot, the driver, closes the coach doors. "We can't go yet! People are missing!" A grey-haired woman from one of the back seats clambers down, reappears a few minutes later with three more women. "Another five minutes," she begs. "There's a crisis in one of the flats."

Drive off at sixteen minutes past five, miss a turning but that only delays us a couple of minutes. Third stop King's Cross. Magnolia and the rest of our group get on. Fourth stop Portland Place. Have to hang around, but not very long, for a member of the lab group who had an urgent errand. An urgent message at this early hour? Dot drives across the Thames and along circuitous side streets slowly burgeoning to life to our fifth stop, in Camberwell.

We're off. The rain splashes. The trees bow in the wind. The coach moves at a steady speed on the flat but crawls uphill. Solomon diagnoses various mechanical faults, any one of which could prove fatal. Rupert's brought a copy of the *Independent* with tips for shopping in Boulogne. Solomon recommends wines and cheeses we should stock up on. Some of us decide we'd rather wander round the town than drive out to the hypermarket. Sixty miles to Dover. Thirty. Ten.

We reach the embarkation point as the ferry's leaving. The next Sealink crossing isn't till 9.45am, that's another hour and forty five minutes. Angus sleeps. Solomon prowls.

The channel is rough. We manage to conceal from the authorities the fact that one of our group has a Uruguayan passport and no entry visa. Why is it so quiet in Calais? Aha! How could we have forgotten? It's All Saints' Day today and the shops are shut. No need to fret, the new shopping centre in Calais is open. But we've booked a meal in Boulogne. If we leave Boulogne early, there'll be time to shop in Calais.

At Boulogne we lose first the tenants, then the lab group. Dot drops us at a *brasserie* in the old town and kips down in the coach. I thought we'd booked dinner in the evening. No, in this country dinner is at noon. The *brasserie* is patronised exclusively by British day trippers - there must be at least a hundred of us. A huge-girthed, star-and-striped T-shirted, pinafored, straw-boatered *monsieur* offers us a four course set meal for the price of a three course set meal and everyone except Solomon and me takes him up on it. Baguettes, herb butter, serve-yourself *hors d'oeuvres* from a chariot washed down by red and white wine. Full already. Mussels washed down by red and white wine. Steak or plaice with *vegetales provençales* and chips washed down by red and white wine.

Mon Dieu! Four o'clock. Time to leave for Calais. We had to wait for everyone else this morning. Let them wait for us now. Hugo goes off to tell Dot we'll be late. Champagne ice cream in miniature champagne bottles. A cheeseboard the size of a satellite dish. Solomon works out how much we each owe and when the bickering dies down it turns out that he was right. Forego coffee and hurtle to the coach, umbrellas aloft, wedges of cheese in our pockets.

Calais again. The temperature's plummeted. I'm exhausted and shivering. Dot kips down in the coach. There isn't nearly enough time to see the new shopping centre properly. Stagger out with bulging bags. Beer - we're allowed 200 25cc bottles each - goes into the luggage hold at the side of the coach. *Beaujolais, brioches, brie, cognac, crème de cassis, camembert*, coffee, raspberry vinegar, walnut oil and life-sized dolls for the grandchildren go into the back. Some of the other passengers are even tiddlier than our lot. It's early. No danger of missing the ferry - it's just along the road.

We hear a sinister crunching noise. Oh dear, the floor of the side luggage hold has collapsed and beer bottles are strewn along the road behind us. Rivulets of muddy beer are flowing towards the gutters. With one or two others I pick up unbroken bottles, carry them to the coach, stuff them into the back, jam them under the seats. A local resident lends me a broom and supervises as I sweep shards of glass off the road, with frequent breaks to let cars and coaches pass on their way to the ferry.

Get off the coach at the customs, all except the sleeping Angus, and unload the back luggage hold to get at our bags. Dot's rubbing my bag down with tissues for some reason.

The channel is rougher than it was this morning. Drinks fly off the tables. My stomach's churning violently. Customs once more at our end. Magnolia is stopped but, overwhelmed by the odour of her tripe pâtè, the customs officer waves her on as he holds his breath to keep from retching.

Collection for Dot. Poor lady's had a tough day. She announces that the first stop will be Camberwell then Portland Place then Swiss Cottage then Finsbury Park and lastly King's Cross. Magnolia wants to know why her stop, King's Cross, is last. Because, says Dot.

At Swiss Cottage Dot starts wiping my bag with tissues again. It's not oil, is it? Yes. So all those stains on my clothes are oil too? I'm afraid so. It's after one in the morning. I'm cold, dirty, hungry and tired and I still have to lug my stuff about a mile home.

"I bet you don't organise another trip to Boulogne in a hurry," I say to Magnolia.

"Why not?" she rasps. "Everyone enjoyed themselves except you."

Travel Issues

New York, before 911 (photo: Peter Bolderson)

911
Barry Needoff (2001)

The world changed on Tuesday September 11, and at once our perception of what was certain, and what was risky, changed with it. Travelling by air, in the "secure" conditions of the Western world, suddenly became fraught with previously unimaginable risk.

Reeling from shock and newfound fear, the world of air travel, previously borne aloft on its own confidence, if not the most secure of financial foundations, began to look very shaky indeed. The United States market was the hardest hit, for air travel there is - or was - accepted as a normal part of day-to-day transport, much as we might use buses or trains.

The effects of these terrorist acts precipitated a crisis in the airline industry, which has spread far beyond the USA.

The airline industry has not, in recent times, been enjoying the best of health, and what happened on September 11 exposed the weaknesses in the industry as a whole. Whilst costs for insurance, additional security and fuel went up in the immediate aftermath, passenger confidence, the willingness to travel and thus booking revenue fell away sharply. A global airline industry cash crisis developed literally overnight.

The major victims are the "flag carriers" or major national airlines, such as British Airways, BMI (British Midland), Swissair, Aer Lingus, Sabena and KLM on this side of the Atlantic; American Airlines, Delta, Continental and United Airlines in the USA. Most of these airlines are dependent on long-haul, transatlantic business travel and much of this has simply disappeared, with the combined loss of business confidence in general, and business travel in particular.

The effects have been immense, with aircraft taken out of service, schedules cut and over 100,000 job losses made or planned. Secondary businesses - airport authorities, plane makers, the wider tourist industry - have all been hit.

The part played in this by the wider economy, in the USA and Europe, should not be forgotten. Growth has been slowing for some time; certain parts of the British and American economies have been in recession for several months, further reducing the demand in the lucrative business travel sector, on which these airlines depend. With less money in people's pockets and the threat of job losses, demand for flying may decline further.

Whilst the United States' administration has looked kindly on requests from their own airlines for financial aid, the picture in Europe was, initially, not so rosy. A paradox arose: the American airlines are private enterprises and may receive Federal funding; European airlines are largely state-owned, but the European Commission forbade state aid to its airlines.

Swissair and Sabena hover perilously close to bankruptcy, but it is a mistake to think that this is all due to recent events - Swissair had been through one cash crisis already in 2001, and was attempting to divest itself of its subsidiary companies in a bid to regain solvency.

The future for "flag carriers" such as these is far from certain. Born in an age where national pride meant investing in modern aircraft at the taxpayers' expense, the uncertainties of the free market (the "Open Skies" policy) in the modern age must surely spell the end for the smaller national carriers.

Can there really be a need for every single European country to offer its own direct flights to New York, Chicago, Los Angeles...? A BBC report claims that the Belgian government may relaunch Sabena as a short-haul carrier. The future for Swissair remains uncertain as current proposals suggest that its European routes will be reduced by a third and handed over to its subsidiary, Crossair. Will the current airline alliances ("Oneworld", "Star Alliance", etc.) turn, *de facto*, into multinational airlines?

Some signs of flexibility from Brussels mean that some European state carriers are now being offered support in the form of compensation for lost passenger revenue in the immediate aftermath of the attacks when US airspace was closed, and some subsidy towards their increased security and insurance costs.

The flag carriers are also being offered some flexibility in the application of rules governing their rights to retain airport take-off and landing slots. Normally, the rule is "use it or lose it", but state airlines are being allowed to retain their rights to these slots for next summer even if they have relinquished them in response to current reduction in traffic.

All this has infuriated the "Low Cost" carriers, who continue to thrive. Flexible in their market offerings and with no exposure to the transatlantic market, they simply piled on the adverts and slashed fares to keep flying. In the immediate aftermath of the terrorist attacks, Go, Ryanair and EasyJet vied for customers still brave enough to fly, with fares as low as £1 return (plus taxes) to European destinations. As a result, their carryings were reportedly hardly affected.

Whistling in a graveyard? Maybe...but it's an ill wind that blows someone some good, as these low-cost carriers try to expand by bidding for slots at Gatwick, suddenly vacated by the flag carriers. It's worth remembering that these airlines are still subject to the increased costs affecting the airline industry as a whole, but may find unexpected advantages with higher demand for short-haul flying and possibly an unexpected supply of cheaper aircraft available for lease.

And what of the future for the charter airlines? In Britain, these are largely linked to the fortunes of their parent companies - the vertically-integrated tour-operating concerns such as Thomson Travel Group (Britannia), First Choice (Air 2000), jmc and Airtours. These carriers sit awkwardly between the low cost operators, which were largely unaffected, and the flag carriers which have been very badly hit.

North America is not a high-volume charter flight destination, but tour-operating groups such as First Choice estimate that the immediate effects of September 11 cost it £10m, and are seeking cost-cutting measures across their group businesses including their airline. The same is true across the other tour-operating groups.

The wider, macro-economic climate will determine the prospects for the charter carriers and their parent companies. If there is a recession, or an extended war, then demand for holidays - especially expensive, long-haul ones - will fall. It seems at the time of writing that the UK's leading tour operators have taken the decision to trim the amount of capacity they will be offering this winter and next summer.

This also applies - but to a lesser extent - for the low-cost carriers. EasyJet's September carryings showed a 3% dip on August's, but were in fact up 27% on September 2000, in line with its year-on-year increase. EasyJet report carrying 7.12m passengers in the year ended September 2001, with load factors of 83%; they anticipate a £35m profit this year.

With the uncertainties besetting flag carriers and the charter carriers, will 2002 be the year in which the low-cost carriers make even greater inroads into the holiday market? Leisure flying - packaged or otherwise - is a discretionary purchase, built upon high disposable income and consumer confidence. An economic downturn will mean less of both and a reluctance to spend scarce cash on a holiday or a quick flight, and the major tour operators will react accordingly with reduced supply and firmer prices. The very short-term prospects are good, for bargain hunters. Go now whilst there is still money to be had and bargain fares and holidays to be bought. Next summer will surely see reduced holiday capacity, fewer charter flights and less scope for bargains.

In the aftermath of September 11, someone asked my opinion of whether she should fly to Spain. True, the airline world is now perceived as a riskier place, but in Europe we have been sensitive to the risks of terrorism - and have reacted accordingly - for some time. I suggested that she should go, be prepared for extra airport security, but still go and enjoy herself. The terrorists of this world will have won if we all remained locked in our homes. In Salman Rushdie's words, "Don't be terrorised. Don't let fear rule your life. Even if you are scared."

Room for One
Heather Wankling (2002)

"Be careful, they'll rob you in Chile," the Argentinian *señora* on the bus told me.

"There are robbers in Argentina as well," responded her companion, a Chilean.

"Yes, but Chile has many more," came the response emphatically, putting an end to all argument.

Being cautioned to take care happens a lot when you travel on your own, especially in countries where machismo is rife. The southern Argentinians warned me of the northern Argentinians (as if anything were possible "up there"), the northern Argentinians warned me of the Brazilians and the Chileans, and even the locals warned me to watch out in Lima!

Usually it is done in a nice way, with genuine concern, but some people (often other travellers) seem to delight in passing on horror stories - they relish telling you how rough the town you're heading towards (and they've just come from) is!

Even as my bus approached Rio de Janeiro, I was mentally planning my escape route out of the city, with mounting anxiety. A North American I had met the previous week had told me in much detail just how bad the crime was there. But, of course, Rio was magnificent - the beaches were gorgeous, away from the shanty areas the city was clean and safe and it was one of the most easy-going places in Brazil.

For me, the pros of travelling alone have always outweighed the cons. For example, I am now a great advocate of the total immersion method of learning a language. In six months in Mexico, alone with my dictionary, my evening-class Spanish progressed in leaps and bounds.

In week one, I attempted a question in halting Spanish with an accent so atrocious that the hotel receptionist didn't even recognise what language I was speaking! A few months later, I was using the phone, reading the newspapers and even managing to crack a joke or two.

I love the spontaneous way people will strike up conversations with a solo traveller, whether it is:

"Good afternoon, it's a nice day, what country do you come from?" (in Argentina)

"Hey you! How many children have you got? My God, you're not married, but how old are you?" (Brazil - I'm 35, and in Brazil would probably be a grandmother!)

"How long does it take to get to England on a bus?" (Mexico)

The Mexicans also had a lovely habit of calling out to me *guerrita*, which means little blondie. "Come here, little blondie", "Where do you come from, little blondie?" At least I think that's what they were saying. The only similar word in the dictionary was *guarrita* - dirty pig - so I like to think it was the former!

Travelling on your own means you often end up with less pleasant accommodation than couples, although the up-side is that if a place is full, and it is getting late, people are often loath to turn you away. Consequently I have slept in a shower in high season when the hostel was so full that others were camping on the roof!

I have also checked into a cheap but nice-looking place in a Mexican port, only to discover when I left that most of the rooms were rented on an hourly basis! That explained the footsteps and slamming doors all through the night; and, on more than one occasion, I have chosen a hotel, reassured by the pleasant motherly-looking lady sitting knitting behind reception, only to return later in the evening to find her replaced by a moustachioed *bandido* with a bandana and a scar on his face, cleaning his finger nails with the tip of a huge machete.

I have met some great fellow travellers (and a few obnoxious ones), and forged some good friendships - more than I ever have during several years sitting in an office behind a computer daydreaming. Of course, it is good to have other people around sometimes, because there are moments which you'd like to share with someone else - waking in the middle of the night to find the bedroom walls shaking after a particularly violent explosion from nearby Mount Arenal, and watching the streams of lava pour down the volcano, glowing brilliant red against a pitch-black backdrop; or the spectacle of a Southern-hemisphere sky when you are miles away from any light pollution - high above the clouds in the Chilean desert or deep in the Ecuadorian jungle; or the night we sat in a small Mexican town watching tracer bullets streak across the sky in the distance, as the Zapatista guerrillas performed night manoeuvres.

Memories like that stay with me long after I have forgotten the minor irritants of travel - lugging a parcel around for five days looking for a post office which was open, or trying to get through US immigration at 5am. As I queued for two hours after a tiring ten-hour flight, I was no longer surprised at how many Mexicans risk swimming the Rio Grande to get into the United States. I think I'd almost rather risk the swim than face that queue again!

At the moment, I have only been home a couple of months and am on a high from my last trip. I still feel a bit lost without my money belt around my waist and my passport at hand, and I have to remind myself that there is no need to carry a toilet roll with me everywhere I go!

In times of trouble the Victorians would open the Bible at random and look for apposite words of comfort on whatever page they came across; they called this the *Sortes Virgilianae*. For times when the post-travel blues strike I have developed my own version, which I play with an atlas. Just looking at all those countries still waiting for me to visit is guaranteed to lift my spirits.

Statue of Kuan Yin, above Hue in Vietnam (photo: June Keeble)

Should I Care?
John Keeble (2003)

The beauty of Kuan Yin, the goddess of compassion, rises 60ft pure white against the blue of the sky, captivating the mind and the camera lens near Hue in central Vietnam. A few miles away, a child lies deformed and helpless, a new victim of Western chemical warfare 30 years ago. Should I care?

To the north-west, in the Phonsavan province of Laos, the senses are absorbed by the mysterious, eponymous jars on the Plain of Jars. Half an hour away, a 12-year-old girl slowly dies - the youngest of seven victims - with her heart ripped from her chest because her village is so poor that its men have been trying to get the explosives from a live 500lb bomb so they can sell the scrap metal. OK, so what has that got to do with travellers?

What are we doing when we visit other countries, other cultures, other tragedies?

Is it enough to admire Kuan Yin, ponder the centuries of vanished pot carvers?

And not just in those places, either. What are we doing in Nagasaki or Dresden; do we care in our comfortable hotel that the genocidal ferocity of our ancestors in Tasmania ended with the last Aborigine being stuffed and kept in a museum; are we happy to enjoy the pleasures of the Amazon without concern for the vanishing jungle, disappearing animals and the tribal cultures under strain; can we stomach the hideously cruel means of getting meat on our plates?

In there somewhere is the first clue to what kind of people we are, what kind of travellers we make.

This is an issue of care. Forget the fact that you loved the restaurant, had a few days in an island paradise, were wowed by the beauty of the sunset over the savannah. That's all OK: you are entitled to enjoyment and that's your payoff for transferring your hard-earned pounds from the UK to someone else's economy.

Beyond that, generally, how aware are you of the people, the animals and the environment?

I find the process is gradual: some I think I know through research before going, some I think I understand while I am there and some I think I catch on to during the months and years after I return.

Like the children of Hue: more than a year after my visit, an article caught my eye in the *Guardian Weekend* as a timely reminder while Iraqi children were dying of cancers caused by depleted uranium shell debris from the first Gulf War.

It was not a surprise. I had been thinking about travelling into the Agent Orange areas of Laos six months earlier and was wondering what I would find there. And probably there was little I could do except spread the word, help a little to get people to open their eyes and their hearts to what the rich world has been doing to the poor world for…for how long? Since the slave trade plundered Africa? Before then? But for us, for our generations, since more recent colonial and post-colonial times.

Of course, it is not just the tragedies and difficulties to be witnessed. How much of the country's culture should we absorb, try to understand? Everything fits together, everyone makes sense as a picture that explains and informs.

We all survive that way and to get a glimpse of another culture's mind and soul is deeply rewarding in what it tells you about yourself as much as the people you are visiting.

For example, to travel in Thailand or Laos without some idea of living Theravada Buddhism is like travelling without a map: you can do it, but you miss so much on the way. And, for me, it comments on my life and the people in it, my way of seeing the world and, in the process, throws off the cloak of normality that usually stops me questioning the basis of my life.

Another interesting insight is the nature of people's relationship to the realities of their lives: how they can live with hope when they have to send out their children in bomblet-littered countryside to hunt for a frog or bird, themselves almost driven to extinction in the area, as a little extra protein for their rice and vegetables.

In the West, the Myanmar government is defined as an evil regime, but the bulk of the people happily go on sorting out the necessities of their lives and the same seems to be true generally throughout the countries I have visited. If you apply a Buddhist idea to explain life's hardships in Myanmar, it is their karma and they make merit to improve this life and the next; in another country, you might explain it differently

Plain of Jars, Laos (above) and some of its victims (photos: June and John Keeble)

but, in catching the flow of the people's mind and seeing the explanation, you will find their realities (how they marry the circumstances with their patterns of explanations).

It is rewarding to talk to people, even when it is difficult for reasons of language...to give a little of yourself, to interest and entertain people with your strange foreignness, to interact instead of falling into the trap of mere voyeuristic observing.

And it is hugely worthwhile to give to good causes like the rebuilding of a temple, the running of a school, the rescue of animals, the saving of people from one of the many awful risks that we never have to face. A little for everyone is good...the price of a drink, a little more if you can afford it or you have a special interest or sympathy.

Often you will be invited to sign a gifts book to show worldwide support for the project. Sometimes help can be in the form of purchases: in Luang Prabang, we bought Buddha necklaces as gifts for our friends; near Angkor Wat, we visited a school for young craftspeople and bought a beautiful wood carving for ourselves...

In the style of the people, I enjoy joining the lives of Thais and Laotians especially. Travelling by bus in Laos, for example, is a social experience and waiting six hours for a bus that might or might not be going is something to accept - and the sense of community with the other people waiting is something to be enjoyed. We sat waiting at Savannakhet bus station in southern Laos all day and, gradually, we were absorbed into the crowd - a companionable silence of someone deliberately sitting with us, the children wanting some kind of contact, an English speaker interpreting another's history through his collection of photographs which seemed to show his two women and assorted kids...and then realising that they, too, were sitting along the row, looking older than the pictures, but nonetheless recognisable.

There are times, like that, when you realise how much you do care about the people of the country you are visiting. And you really do not like them living with the horrors of war that rip their hearts out. And you come back to the UK and tell everyone.

Perhaps, in the end, that is one of the most valuable things you can achieve when you travel. You see, understand and return to slice little gaps in the curtain of people's immediate concerns...to show a bigger picture to many who would care if they knew the truth of others' lives.

A La Recherche des Journées Perdues
Mike Cruickshank (2001)

STOLEN, on Waterloo Station:- One black holdall containing some French francs, medication and a small assortment of books including a hard-covered notebook which had, for a number of years, done duty as a travel diary.

My immediate reaction was that I must have somehow dropped it somewhere on the station. I started to retrace my steps to look for it. The first person I met had actually seen the bag being snatched, but had been too shocked to raise the alarm.

By this time, I was in a state of choked disbelief myself. After decades of thief-free travelling, I had finally been caught out by a bag snatcher before I had even left the country.

However, no insurmountable damage had been done: tickets and passport were safe, the police were informed, cash was topped up from the nearest hole in the wall and the couple of days in Paris went ahead.

It was only at home some days later, filling in the insurance claim (I had smugly thought at the time that buying insurance cover was a waste of money), that I started thinking.

Virtually everything but the diary could be reduced to a cash price, even those which had been gifts and therefore with a sentimental value. But how does one put a value on a diary?

To anyone stealing or finding it, it would be of no value or interest whatsoever. To me, this diary, covering as it did most of my travels over a period of nearly ten years, was priceless.

I could retrace most of the journeys in broad outline from memory, but to do so in reality would cost thousands. How, though, can one ever recapture those magic first impressions of a place?

What about the people one meets over the years?

The magnificently bearded down, but not quite out, character in a café in Evora, Portugal? He was having a vigorous conversation with an invisible companion and looked for all the world like an Old Testament prophet having a row with the Almighty, and losing.

There was the deaf-mute in Vigo who would do rough (very rough) pen portraits for the price of a drink: a likeable character who seemed to be well known and liked along that stretch of Vigo seafront.

Events?

An open air play performed at night with the cathedral of Santiago de Compostela as a floodlit backdrop. A dance routine in the same square performed by South American Indians. Sitting in a café over coffee and croissants, watching the marriage of the King of Spain's daughter on television. A stark contrast to the funeral of Princess Diana, which had taken place only weeks earlier.

At least I think it had. I can't now check it against my diary.

Then there are the places I may never find again.

A number of "Hammer Film" style bars (three, I think) in various parts of Galicia. You may know the sort of thing - rough stone walls lined with bottles, some of them very dusty - and customers equally rough and dusty. Rows of hams and sausages dangling from the wooden ceiling.

One even sported a whistling toilet out in the backyard (whistling toilet? no lock on the door). There was even a large stroppy-looking dog on duty outside, presumably to ensure that no-one escaped with the sheets of torn-up newspaper hanging from a nail behind the door; a warning to all those getting caught short travelling off the beaten track.

The bits I'd like to forget?

A holiday in Galicia when it rained every day for a fortnight? I have always maintained that anyone who can't amuse themselves on a wet day isn't fit to travel. Fourteen days of the stuff was pushing it more than somewhat.

Then there was a hotel in Abbeville. "Hotel" proved to be rather a grand term for a backpackers' flop shop. The bar across the road sported a barman who seemed in mortal terror of serving the hairy foreigner with the bad French.

He went running to the patron every time I asked for a drink. He understood well enough when I came to settle up: too well, he tried to short change me by ten francs.

Was it Dr Johnson who said that the greatest sight that a Scotsman can see is the road to England? The greatest sight that this one saw on the following day was the railway out of Abbeville that morning.

And the future? Keep going, exercising a bit more care and attention, and make a copy of any diary entries as soon as possible after I get home. I might even go hi-tech and buy a decent camera if the insurance company stumps up enough.

Travel In Brief

Vietnamese jungle scene (photo: John Piper)

Travel in Brief

NIGHT INTRUDERS (Jeff Jowers, 2004)

On our last night, we were back in Buenos Aires. Our hostel only had double rooms free in its brand-new annexe around the corner. There was nobody else there. It was a work in progress really, paint and tools everywhere, but the room was finished and there was hot water, so it was fine. Actually, it was quite fun - like having our own apartment. Or at least it was, until we heard footsteps downstairs.

"What's that noise?" Cath said. There weren't even any staff in the annexe.

"Maybe they've come in to do some more decorating," I said.

She looked at the clock.

"It's 4.49 on a Sunday morning."

So we lay there, listening for sounds, clues. It was pitch black in our room, except for four huge eyeballs, a bit like Scooby and Shaggy in a haunted cellar. What could they be looking for? There was nothing to steal. Did they think the place was empty? Or would they realise we were there? Which was worse? What should we do if they tried our door?

I considered our defence options - two small Swiss Army knives, some duct tape and a souvenir cow-hoof ashtray. Often it would be silent for minutes on end, but then the noises would start again, voices too. But they didn't come upstairs and, as far as we could tell, they didn't do much at all.

By morning we'd managed to get some sleep. We woke to beautiful breakfast smells which, combined with the daylight, gave us the courage to leave the room. Nothing had been touched. I went up to the roof, to see if there was a way in or out across the top. From there I had a view of the landing and, on the floor below, the source of the smells, a bakery...

They'd been baking bread.

PEOPLE AT LAST (Glen Strachan, 2001)

Ponder a journey that starts in London and takes you to Australia, where the "evil empire" once enslaved the indigenous, forced their conversion to Christianity and treated the Aborigine population as savages. Think about the fact that only in recent years has the Aborigine been reclassified by the Australian government as a person. Prior to that they were "regulated" as flora and fauna. Maybe when a moral standpoint comes closer to home, the view is a little different.

Colonial goverment, Commonwealth control and the sad influence of the European-based Christian churches has made the indigenous Australian the victim of a systematic regime of cruelty, the "slave-legacy" of which is even today clear for all to see. Consider our sad track record as we prepare to judge others from the "ethical safe-haven" of Cool Britannia's cosmopolitan London of 2001.

THE RASPUTIN GANG (Tim Grimes, 1998)

I joined Sunday morning service at the nearby Russian Orthodox church, one of many. The church was full (presumably of the Russians still living in Vilnius). The incantation of the worshippers was moving and the thick air of incense was migraine-inducing. The congregation bowed and genuflected with almost aerobic frequency. The priest, wearing a cape of gold and deep pink, with matching tall spherical hat, was assisted by half a dozen similarly clad acolytes all with an uncanny Rasputin resemblance, although one looked more like Billy Connolly. The church was adorned with paintings and more icons than a fully tooled-up Word for Windows.

As I left, I ran the gamut of begging, toothless old ladies, whose entreaties I had to resist as the smallest change I had was a note worth the equivalent of £12.42. I wasn't too worried by the imprecations and curses which this attracted. The last time I was cursed, it was by a Hungarian gypsy violinist who thought I had under-tipped him, the curse missed, flew out of the window and caused a road accident outside.

SALT (Jeff Jowers, 2004)

Uyuni gets such a big build-up, we were sure we were going to be disappointed. Not one person who's been there doesn't list it amongst the best places they've ever been.

Actually that isn't 100% accurate. Uyuni itself is a dreadful place, freezing cold and with nothing at all to do. It's expensive too (cigarettes £1 instead of 50p) and that's because it's a seller's market - there's just nowhere else nearby you could possibly go to buy anything. The only reason anyone goes there is to take a journey into the nearby salt flats and beyond. For $85 each (an absolute fortune in Bolivia) you get a 4x4 Jeep with a driver/guide and four days' food (simple) and accommodation (basic). There's no other way to do it, though - it really is like the end of the world.

After an hour on the first morning we reached the edge of the salt flat. There was once a huge sea there, but when the Andes were pushed up all the water went, and left the salt behind. I'm talking hundreds of square miles, of just white. Without a cloud in the sky, the reflection from the sun is dazzling. You have to keep touching the ground to remind yourself it isn't snow. Under normal circumstances it must be impressive enough. This year, however, the rains had been heavier than usual, and this makes it even more surreal. All morning, and for half the afternoon, we drove through up to 50cm of water. On every horizon were the surrounding mountains, reflected perfectly in the water below. It looked like we were on an iced lake.

It's beautiful. Even so, I was wondering why we needed four days. As it turned out, the other days took us out of the salt flats and on to one spectacular sight after another. We saw 1,200-year-old cacti. We would drive over the brow of a hill and see, beside us, the top of a 5,000-metre mountain. We went past a desert full of towering rocks with such bizarre shapes that they're called the Salvador Dali rocks. There is a lake which, rich in iron, magnesium, algae and plankton, is completely red. Another one, full of different minerals, is reputedly green. When we got there it didn't look very green, because there was a perfect reflection in it of the volcano behind. Within five minutes, the wind had got up, the surface of the lake was broken, the reflection had gone and there it was. Green. There were hot springs. Sulphur geysers. And when the Jedi warriors appeared on the horizon...OK, they didn't really, but if they had it wouldn't have seemed out of the ordinary.

CARIBBEAN DREAM (Gillian Kennedy, 2004)

The night we got to Tobago Cays, by happy coincidence, Shane's father heard on the radio that there was going to be a total eclipse of the moon that night. No-one on the surrounding boats seemed to know about it, as all the other yachts moored there had their lights out when the eclipse started around 1am. So we had one of the tiny islands totally to ourselves. We were able to lie back on the soft white sand, close to some palm trees, and watch the moon slowly disappear and the stars shine so much brighter than normal without the moon's light. We were able to see the "sparkles in the sea" while we waited for the moon to reappear. These were phosphorescent phyto-plankton and, when we scooped them up in our hands with some sea water, they appeared all to be different shapes.

The next morning some of the boat boys offered to catch us lobster and duly reappeared a while later with barbecued lobster (probably crayfish really, but very tasty). These we ate with some lovely salads prepared by the men on board and accompanied by champagne. Lobster and champagne brunch on a yacht in the Caribbean, the morning after a total eclipse of the moon - during January. That's the life!

BEHIND BARS IN EL SALVADOR (Terry Gibbon, 2000)

The taxi driver took us to a very primitive hotel and we could not understand that it was only $10 for the night. We decided to make the best of it for the night but, when it became obvious that the receptionist was illiterate and we could not make him understand that we wanted a taxi for the next morning, we put ourselves on the street. What went wrong when that hotel advertised that they spoke English?

We carried our entire luggage in a temperature of 95°F, found a taxi and asked the driver to take us to a hotel where English was spoken. As we were obviously going to have language trouble again, I went into the nearby barber's shop that happened to be there and asked them if they could help with the taxi. When I asked the barber for his help, he said he would walk with me to an English-speaking hotel. To my amazement, he took me back to our first hotel and banged on the next door, which looked like a private house, but turned out to be the hotel I had originally booked. They are so concerned with security in these countries that they barricade themselves in with steel doors and grilles so it is difficult to identify them. The original hotel had given itself the same name, so that they pinch some of the customers from next door.

LAST WILDERNESS (Margaret Walker, 2002)

To get the atmosphere of this wild region of peat bogs and moorland, take a narrow, gated road from Newbiggin to Daddry Shield (Co. Durham). It helps if you have a companion to hop out of the car, chase the sheep away (if any remain after this terrible scourge of foot and mouth) and open and close the gates for you. Only the most remote areas are still gated; elsewhere you will rattle noisily over cattle grids. Up here there are few signs of habitation, as the population plummeted when the lead mining ceased. If you are lucky, you will see flocks of green plover, or a hen harrier searching for prey, startle a hare or a whirring grouse and hear the haunting cry of the curlew. You are unlikely to meet another car on this road. Stop, roll down the windows, breathe and listen to the silence. Better still, walk. This is England's last wilderness.

FLYING IN THE FALKLANDS (Sally Branston, 2004)

As there are very few paved roads and many of the tracks are rutted and adversely affected by weather conditions, flying is often the only way to get about, particularly if you wish to travel a long distance or visit one of the outlying islands. As a military spouse, I was fortunate to be eligible to use three of the available means of air transport: the Falkland Islands Government Air Service (FIGAS), with their small, red, Islander aircraft; the Sikorsky helicopters of British International Helicopters (BRINTEL); and once, a Royal Air Force Sea King helicopter. Only the first of these is available to the general public.

Flying with FIGAS is a very different experience from flying with a big airline in this country as it's really an air taxi service. When you initially book your ticket, you state your dates of travel and the places you want to go from and to, and yes, you have to give your weight. I wonder how many people lie about this? You also have to state if you're carrying anything heavy such as golf clubs (there are indeed golf courses on the Falklands) or a box of groceries if you're going to stay in self-catering accommodation at your destination.

Then, the night before your flight, you listen to the Falkland Island Broadcasting Service (FIBS) and at an appointed time, the flight schedules are read out. This is when you learn what time your aircraft is going to come and pick you up as your name is read out over the air. You also learn the names of your fellow travellers and who is going where and with whom. There are no secrets on the Falklands! People speculate avidly when they learn that the doctor is paying a visit to an island or a farm. They listen for his flight times to gauge the nature and severity of the illness by the length of the visit. I am told that only social workers paying a visit where children are involved are allowed to withhold their names, so there is no chance for anyone else to have an affair or sneak off for a dirty weekend!

HAWAII (Martin Snow, 2001)

Early next day I hit the Volcanoes National Park, where there are hundreds of craters, the main one, Kilauea Crater, being ten miles in diameter with a road around it along which the tourist coaches cruise. This has other craters within it, the most recent one in 1982. In the National Park there is an excellent Visitors' Center and Observatory, with lots of things to do such as climbing through lava tubes, examining steam vents, and walking across devastation trails and smoking craters. The active volcanic area is 15 miles from here along the windy Chain of Craters Road built over previous lava flows. No tour buses go along this route, so there is little other traffic. The road ends abruptly near the coast, where a lava flow covered it about ten years ago. The same lava flow also covered villages for the next ten miles along the road. Here you can walk up on to the lava, but there are Park Rangers stationed at the top. They attempt to deter all but the most determined adventurers from walking the four miles to get to the active lava flow. They mention the walk is over jagged, razor sharp, pot-holed, undulating old lava, with no marked route and in the searing heat of the day. Those they can't deter are advised on what provisions to take.

After starting, I felt uneasy for the first hour as I saw no-one else on the trek, but eventually caught up with a few others, and saw a few more in the distance ahead. It was just that I had left it a bit late to set off to get there by nightfall. Later I caught up with several more high-spirited trekkers on their way to see the best natural New Year's Eve firework display on offer. Going as fast as I could, it still took two hours of exhausting walking over the rough terrain. The drinking water came in handy, as it was very hot and sweaty on the exposed and baking landscape. Some lava gave way or cracked off underfoot. Trenches and holes were everywhere, waiting to trap the ankle of the unwary. At long last, the smoke from the molten lava became visible, then approaching you heard crackling and felt the wall of heat hit you. The Park Ranger had warned that the edge of the molten lava was hard to distinguish by daylight, so you had to listen for crackles coming from the solidifying rock. It was much easier as night fell, as the molten lava then glowed bright fiery red. Sunset takes only ten minutes here, as it is so near the

Equator. After seeing in the New Year watching the brilliant colours of flowing rock, it was time to think about returning. I wasn't sure how much battery power I had left in my torch, and didn't want to get stuck on the way back having to wait for daylight because my battery was flat, so I joined a family of mainland Americans for the return journey. The parents were working as nurses in a local hospital for a year and their teenage daughters raced each other over the rugged solidified lava, as surefooted as mountain goats. They knew there was a satellite due to cross the sky at a certain time and we could see it quite clearly. By moonlight the recent lava shone silvery, and when the moon went behind a small cloud the sky was full of bright stars. I had never seen so many with the naked eye.

CHRISTMAS IN NEPAL (Marie Fogg, 2004)

Next day was Christmas Eve, which I spent in Kathmandu with newfound friends. In the evening we went for a meal and had a visit from Santa. When I woke in the morning I thought I heard Bing Crosby singing *White Christmas*. But no, it was the owners of the guesthouse playing tapes to try and make us feel at home. They even wrapped white toilet roll round the trees to make it look like snow. I spent most of the day thinking about my family back home and wondering what they were doing. In the evening we went to a barbecue. It was the first time I had eaten water buffalo and goat.

LIFE ON MARS (Tony Wallbank, 2005)

There are some volcanic cones here called "rootless cones" that have only been found in Iceland and on Mars. These are formed when hot lava flows over and through soggy ground and explodes. The resulting cones are then fed by more lava flowing along the same route. The lake at Mývatn is shallow and these cones stick out of the water giving a surreal landscape. It is an active area and Krafla, the big volcano in the area, last erupted from 1975 to 1984. There are steam vents all over the place and, in one place, one of them has sprung up beside the road, blocking the view. We were surprised to see a digger coming at us through the cloud of steam. It was actually spreading more volcanic ash on the road, which was being re-built following the collapse of its predecessor further up the hill.

On the return journey a couple of hours later the way was blocked by a huge lorry dumping more material on the road. They were digging black volcanic ash out of the hillside a few hundred yards away and making the road. We had to wait while the digger roughly spread the stuff out and then we had to drive over the resulting very soft surface. To add to the challenge, it was still all covered in steam and impossible to see if there was anything coming the other way. There are fascinating lava formations in the Mývatn region, including a 2km² area with huge ornate structures including old lava tubes big enough to hold a concert in. One such structure is "the church".

EARS PIERCED WHILE YOU WAIT (Margaret Walker, 1999)

We came across a village festival and stopped to see what was going on. Immediately we were welcomed and ushered forward to the centre of things. Passing two gaudily painted statues of horses and riders (representing the guardian deities of the village) we found the centre of attention to be a small boy whose head was being shaved, the hair then being ceremonially burned on a brass tray.

The next ordeal for him was ear piercing. Apparently this is done as a mutilation so that the gods will be dissuaded from taking the child away from its parents. An earring is then worn by boys up to the age of 12, by which time the gods have presumably lost interest! This did not appear to be a village of poor peasants, but of well-to-do *bourgeois*. I was approached by two charming small boys, pupils at the French *lycée* in Pondicherry, who explained what was going on in perfect French. Their mother wore a dark-blue silk sari and ample amounts of gold jewellery.

At the moment of ear-piercing, loud drumming took place, but the child did not cry, and submitted afterwards to being dressed in a neat outfit of trousers, jacket, shirt and bow tie! On the ground near the stage where the main protagonists were assembled, a rectangle was marked out with small stones. Inside were pairs of clay blobs, apparently representing the family gods, whose names were only known to the individual families. In front of each pair were set out banana leaves, piled with sugar-cane, rice from the recent harvest and pieces of coconut. The coconut is highly prized and signifies the passage of the soul from the cares of this world (the rough outer fibres) through pride and egotism (the hard shell) to the white flesh representing purity. We were also told that the three "eyes" of the coconut represent the three eyes of Vishnu.

STONED FOR LOVE (Jeff Jowers, 2004)

More interesting is the island of Taquile [in Peru]. You can get a boat to the island and stay a night. A guide explains the people's way of life, traditions and beliefs, and you can see ancient houses, burial sites and temples. All money they make from souvenirs, food, lodging etc. is shared amongst the entire community. Inevitably, some households have set up private-enterprise lodging so, to get round this, all the private hostels have to take it in turns to spend their takings on a massive party.

Nobody steals and nobody lies, as this would result in being outcast from society. The girls all speak in whispers, and if a boy fancies a girl he throws small stones at her and hopes she doesn't run away. All couples have a trial period together before getting married - this can include setting up home and even having children. Only when they get married are they committed. It was really fascinating, a proper window on another world. Obviously, tourism is having an effect, and some of the brasher young things now have windows and even radios.

DAY OF THE DEAD (Glen Strachan, 2000)

Many of Mexico's festivals are of Pagan origin but have been co-opted by the Catholic Church over the centuries. A fine instance of this is The Day of the Dead. This celebration of the contribution of one's ancestors invokes inviting their spirits to return (temporarily) to our earthly world where they will be treated with reverence. In pre-Hispanic times, Mexican cultures believed that the cold north winds brought the spirits of the dead back to visit. Festivals were then arranged to honour these spirits.

The conquering Catholic Church realised that erasing such local customs would be impossible and, selecting the Day of the Dead as an important pan-Mexican festival, the Spaniards fused it with All Saints' Day and All Souls' Day. Such synthesis has for generations defined Mexican culture.

Day of the Dead altars are built in homes, decoration varying according to the traditions of each region. In Oaxaca the altar is usually installed on a table with a white cloth and tissue-paper cut-outs. Stalks of sugar cane or bamboo are used to fashion a triumphal arch. This is where the spirit will enter and be welcomed. The altar is decorated with marigolds (the flower of the dead), oil lamps, scented candles, photographs or portraits of the deceased, incense, special sweet bread (*pan de Muerto*), black mole (a local delicacy), sugared figures, candied pumpkin, hot chocolate and seasonal fruits like the little Tejocote apples together with individual items such as a favourite beer or a particular food.

When the altar is completed on the morning of October 31, nothing is touched. The departed soul then returns to our world, takes in the aromas of the altar and seeks out the bereaved. The day ends with a lively family dinner and the deceased depart for another year.

COLUMBO AND THE IRISHMAN (Mike Cruickshank, 2001)

I was pleased to see that my favourite watering hole, a bar / fish restaurant at the end of the beach, was still there and still being run by a disreputable looking version of Lt Columbo, the TV detective. He was a bit fatter in the face than I remembered him, and looked every inch the genial ruffian. It was here that I got talking to an Irishman who had just completed the pilgrimage to Santiago and had carried on the extra miles to Finisterre. (In the Middle Ages, this last bit was sometimes imposed on pilgrims as an extra penance.) He seemed quite shocked to find out that the bus fare between Santiago and Finisterre came to about a fiver, in spite of having taken three days to walk the distance in the pouring rain. How much of this was an Irishism, and how much down to the effects of the pilgrimage I don't know, but there we sat, one of us with more money than sense and the other with more time.

A TASTE OF JEREZ (Beryl Jolliffe, 2004)

We discovered that many places in the region had "de la Frontera" in their name because the actual frontier in that area of Spain had moved several times as a result of Moorish incursions. "Sherry" was the nearest the English could get to pronouncing the Spanish name Jerez! Needless to say we were given a tour of a winery (Tio Pepe) with wine-tasting included, but what we remember chiefly is the small tourist attraction there. In one room full of barrels we were asked to stand still and keep very quiet "because of the livestock". We froze, and looked ahead along the walkway where stood a wineglass with a miniature ladder reaching to the top. After a pause, some small mice ventured out from the barrels to pick up crumbs which were lying there and then a bolder, larger mouse made its way to the ladder, and, after checking carefully that the coast was clear, climbed up and delicately sipped the sherry. Apparently a workman who used to have his sandwiches there found the mice liked crumbs and sherry, so he devised this unusual show.

WHAT THE GUIDE DOESN'T TELL YOU (David Gourley, 2004)

Even on the way down, Zaporozhye had struck me as very Soviet, not a description I'd apply to Kiev, Odessa or Sevastopol. As well as the Dam, we saw the huge statue of Lenin which dominates the quayside. This marks the start of the eponymous Prospekt, the main thoroughfare, which runs inland some half dozen miles or so. Classic Soviet architecture, rather impressive in its own way, lines its entire length - though McDonald's has found its way even here. This felt like a trip through time as well as distance. At one point, we could see through a gap in the buildings a nearby factory, a dinosaur of a place that was absolutely massive with belching chimneys and flares. There was a still clearer view later in the day, as we recommenced our cruise. Lilia, our guide, noticed us looking at it with fascination. "Sometimes," she sighed, "I don't point things out, in the hope people won't notice them."

CUPBOARDS AND CHICKENS (Anne Dearle, 1999)

We stopped at Chicken (population 17), which was an experience not to be missed. I made a beeline for a wooden building labelled "Ladies". The term "building" is used loosely as it was really a sort of cupboard balanced on a slab of concrete, and looking as if it might dislodge itself at any minute. I was rather anxious about the tilt and even more concerned by the fact that the door appeared to be hanging off. I was completely put off when I opened this door to find that there was a double loo inside. There were two lavatory seats side by side with nothing between them, so that two ladies could have sat cosily having a chat whilst relieving themselves. Not for me! I decided I could wait a little longer.

There was a row of wooden shacks housing various shops, the first in line being a gift shop run by a plump and motherly lady who sported a short, but very luxuriant black beard. She tried desperately to interest us all in a variety of slightly doubtful souvenirs, including keyrings and bookmarks that proclaimed "I got laid in Chicken", and something that I thought was a book of matches with the picture of a chicken on the front; it turned out to be a packet of condoms.

ANCESTORS IN THE DEEP FREEZE (Peter Bolderson, 2000)

We visited Fort Yukon one evening, on the Arctic Circle about 150 miles northeast of Fairbanks, flying by Piper Navajo over the White Mountains. The evenings remain light. Four aircraft went together. This is no longer a wooden walled fort of Hudson's Bay trading days but a collection of houses on stilts. Our guide was very open, friendly and self-assured as he drove us about the village in their recently acquired refurbished bus. It had been barged up the Yukon that summer. He took us to the landing place to gaze into the vastness of the Yukon. His brother arrived from a downriver fish camp. We inspected his fish wheel and listened to details of the salmon disaster that year. Driving past the cemetery, he told us that all his recent ancestors were there, good as the day they died, seven foot down in the permafrost, just like a deep freeze. They didn't bother burying their dead until the missionaries came, leaving them out on the tundra or cremating them.

VIETNAM'S RESTAURANT CRITIC (John Piper, 2005)

I am in a canoe gliding down a narrow canal in the heart of the jungle. Many years ago a whole army hid in this jungle and the land was regularly napalmed by offensive forces. Now there are smiling faces as other canoes come down the canal towards us and the vegetation is very lush as we float past. But what is that? Is that a snake I see coiling itself away in the undergrowth?

Later the same day I walked into a restaurant to find a large barbecued toad sitting on the griddle and a menu which included such exotica as "stewed goats penis" and "fried sheep's ovaries" - I decided to stick to wild boar! The restaurant staff were extremely attentive and we had a fabulous time. There were five of us and the bill came to less than £15 - including a bottle of Vietnam spirit and two bottles of very good Vietnamese wine. There was even a floor show in the shape of a giant rat which was attempting to get into the kitchen.

What more could one ask? In the UK the spoilsport health and safety people would have closed it down - you have to go away to see how life really is, get away from the cosmetic nanny state that the UK is rapidly becoming.

Every restaurant should sport a giant rat - at least that way you know that something likes the food.